NARUTO FOREVER

The Unofficial Guide

cocoro books

www.dhp-online.com

cocoro books is an imprint of DH Publishing, Inc.

First Published 2008
Second Published 2008

Compiled by Kazuhisa Fujie, Ivan Rorick

ISBN: 978-1-932897-25-8

Naruto Forever: The Saga Continues

How to Use
In this book, the 17th in the popular Mysteries and Secrets Revealed! anime sourcebook series, you'll find everything you need to know about Naruto and much, much more! And it's so easy to use. Just follow the Naruto code below and within a few hours you'll be a ninjutsu know-it-all.

Questions and Answers
Want to find out why who did what when and where? Then this is the book for you. Continue reading, and you'll find 74 Q&As on every Naruto topic, from the world the characters live and fight in to the weaponry and jutsu their use.

Glossary
When you speak the lingo everything is so much easier. At the back of this book you'll find a comprehensive list of the many Naruto characters, as well as a comprehensive list of ninja techniques.

Keyword Index
Want to go straight to the Land of Lightning? Then start at the alphabetical Keyword Index at the back of this book. There you'll find page links to every character, destination and jutsu in Naruto's world.

Overview

Naruto is a shonen manga by Kishimoto Masashi that has been serialized in *Weekly Shonen Jump* since its 43rd issue in 1999. It is a ninja action comic that centers on a youth named Naruto Uzumaki who aspires to become a top ninja. Rather than focusing on the fundamental ninja duties of assassination and the like, it focuses on the growth of the main character Naruto (who has the Nine-Tailed Demon Fox sealed within him) and portrays the battles of him and his fellow ninja. It has become a hugely popular manga and the second series is currently being serialized. In 2002, a TV anime series was launched that developed into an 85-part original story. In its second series, the show was renamed *Naruto: Shippuden.* This book mainly explains the original manga work, but will occasionally touch upon the anime series as well.

The Naruto story at a glance

The first series

Years before the story commences, the village of Konohagakure is attacked by the Nine Tailed Demon Fox. Before the village is destroyed, its chief at the time, the Fourth Hokage (Fire Shadow), sacrifices his own life to seal the Demon Fox within the body of the infant Naruto, who was born just before the Demon Fox's attack. As Naruto grows up, he aspires to be the next Hokage, becomes a ninja, and competes in the Chunin (Middle Ninja) trials. Naruto gradually awakens the mysterious powers of the Nine Tailed Demon Fox within him, but he is misled during the trials by Orochimaru, a ninja whose intention is to destroy Konohagakure. A coup d'état ensues...

The second series

Two and a half years have passed since the coup d'état in Konohagakure, and Naruto has grown into an exceptional ninja. He is concerned about his close friend Sasuke, and hears that the new chief of ninja village Sunagakure, Gaara, (with whom Naruto developed a rapport during the ninja trials), has been kidnapped by the mysterious organization Akatsuki, which is said to be gathering the tailed demons sealed within Gaara, Naruto and others. It is said that Itachi, elder brother of Naruto's close friend Sasuke and suspected perpetrator of the Uchiha clan massacre, is part of the group. To rescue Gaara and bring Sasuke back to the village, Naruto faces a new battle...

CONTENTS

Overview...4
Contents..5

Secrets of the Ninja...7
Q01   Why do ninja live in shinobi villages?..8
Q02   What are the Five Great Ninja Countries?...10
Q03   What is the relationship between the states and their shinobi villages?.........13
Q04   What was the Great Ninja World War?..15
Q05   How does someone become a ninja?...16
Q06   What are a ninja's duties?...18
Q07   What are the ninja ranks?..20
Q08   What are nukenin and oinin?...22
Q09   What kind of jutsu do the ninja use?..25
Q10   Why is the use of kinjutsu restricted?..28
Q11   What kinds of ningu exist?...30
Q12   What is the chakra that gives the ninja his energy?......................................31
Q13   What are the chakra keitai henka and seishitsu henka?.................................33
Q14   What are Kekkei Genkai?...36

Secrets of Naruto..39
Q15   What is the Nine Tailed Demon Fox sealed within Naruto?............................40
Q16   Who were Naruto's parents?...42
Q17   Why can't Naruto control the Demon Fox within him?...................................44
Q18   Is Naruto a human weapon?..46
Q19   Is Naruto safe using the kinjutsu Kage Bunshin?..48
Q20   Why is Naruto able to quickly recover from his wounds?...............................50
Q21   What kind of jutsu is Naruto's specialty, the Rasengan?...............................52
Q22   Why is Naruto taking on the form of the fox more and more?.........................54
Q23   How did Kakashi recruit Naruto?...56
Q24   What kind of jutsu is the Rasen Shuriken?...59
Q25   Will Naruto die if the spirit of the Demon Fox escapes from him?..................60

Secrets of the Ninja from Konohagakure...61
Q26   When was Konohagakure founded?...62
Q27   Who were the past Hokage?...64
Q28   What kind of person is the current Hokage, Tsunade?...................................67
Q29   Who are the three legendary ninja?...69
Q30   Why did Orochimaru try to destroy Konohagakure?.....................................71
Q31   What is Orochimaru plotting now?..73
Q32   Why did Itachi Uchiha massacre his clan?...76
Q33   Why did Itachi join Akatsuki?...78
Q34   Why is Sasuke Uchiha so caught up in becoming powerful?.........................80
Q35   Why did Sasuke Uchiha leave his village?..81
Q36   Why does Sasuke have wings?..83
Q37   Did Sasuke kill Orochimaru?...85
Q38   Who are the members of the four-man Hebi group formed by Sasuke?...........87

Q39 Why does Tsunade go after Itachi? 89
Q40 Why is Kakashi able to use the Sharingan? 90
Q41 What is the Kikaichu jutsu? 92
Q42 Why is Kiba Inazuka able to change into a beast? 93
Q43 Why is only the main branch of the Hyuga important? 95
Q44 What is Choji's specialty, the Baika jutsu? 97
Q45 What kind of person is Sai? 99
Q46 Who are the Anbu? 101
Q47 What about Asuma Sarutobi and Kurenai? 102
Q48 Why is Shikamaru such a great strategist? 103
Q49 What is Ino's specialty, the Shintenshin jutsu? 105

Mysteries of the Village of Sunagakure 107
Q50 What is the Shukaku inside Gaara? 108
Q51 Is the previous Kazekage responsible for Gaara? 109
Q52 What is Gaara's special Zettai Bogyo technique? 111
Q53 What happens to Gaara if the Shukaku is removed? 113
Q54 Why does Sunagakure view Konohagakure as its rival? 115
Q55 Did Chiyobaa develop the Kairai jutsu? 117
Q56 Who made the puppets that Kankuro uses? 119
Q57 Is Temari the only one to use the giant fan weapon? 120

Secrets of Otogakure 121
Q58 Why does Orochimaru establish the village of Otogakure? 122
Q59 Why does Kabuto Yakushi follow Orochimaru? 124
Q60 Why didn't Kimimaro become Orochimaru's next body? 126
Q61 Why does Kidomaru look like a spider? 127
Q62 What special talents do Sakon and Ukon have? 129
Q63 What special abilities does Jirobo have? 130
Q64 What special powers does Tayuya have? 131

Secrets of Akatsuki 133
Q65 What is Akatsuki's interest in jinchuriki? 134
Q66 How does Akatsuki recruit new members? 136
Q67 How many members does Akatsuki have? 137
Q68 Who is the leader of Akatsuki? 139
Q69 What kind of place is the village of Amegakure? 141
Q70 What is Deidara's specialty? 143
Q71 How did Hidan survive decapitation? 145
Q72 Why does Kakuzu have five hearts? 146
Q73 Who is Madara Uchiha? 148
Q74 Who is the legendary ninja, Sennin Rikido? 149

GLOSSARY 151
Characters 152
Ninjutsu 177

KEYWORD INDEX 188

Chapter 01

Secrets of the Ninja

01 Why do ninja live in shinobi villages?

Naruto is a ninja born and raised in the village of Konohagakure (lit. hidden in the leaves). Konohagakure is part of the Land of Fire, but ninja villages also exist in other countries. Weapons such as missiles and tanks do not exist in Naruto's world. In place of these, the different states train ninja, who function as their military defense. In times of war, ninja act as a military force and do battle.

Because ninja defend their respective countries in this way, each country uses a great deal of its national budget to train and cultivate strong ninja as if it is developing new weaponry. Highly-skilled ninja and their ninjutsu (ninja techniques) are national military secrets. When new ninja are discovered, they are hidden away in villages located in the middle of nowhere, where they live in seclusion, training and developing in secret. These hidden villages are called *shinobi* villages. Most are in remote places like forests in the middle of mountains.

Although they are "ninja" villages, they are

not only inhabited by ninja. Even ninja have to live everyday lives, and people who manage clothing stores, flower shops, and restaurants also live there. The owner of the ramen shop Ichiraku that Naruto likes is a 30-year ramen veteran, not a ninja. However, the family of Ino Yamanaka, a close friend of Sasuke and classmate of Naruto, runs a flower shop, although the father, Inoichi Yamanaka is a ninja. There are others in the ninja villages who, like Inoichi, are ninja but have jobs on the side.

⑤ee Keyword
Konohagakure
Ino
Inoichi

02 What are the Five Great Ninja Countries?

In the world where Naruto lives there is a vast continent, and on it there are various countries, large and small. These countries all train ninja for national defense. However, among them, the Land of Fire, Land of Wind, Land of Lightning and Land of Earth are the principal states, occupying three-quarters of the continent. Including the island nation, the Land of Water, these dominant countries with their powerful ninja are known as the Five Great Ninja Countries.

The northernmost of the five is the Land of Lightning. Kumogakure (lit. hidden among the clouds), headed by the Raikage (Lightning Shadow), is one of its villages. There are many towering mountain ranges, and the roar of thunder can be heard reverberating throughout them. There are also many rivers, which cut through the mountains to create a complex geography.

The Land of Earth boasts the village of Iwagakure (lit. hidden among rocks), headed by the Tsuchikage (Earth Shadow). Desolate rocky landscapes make up much of the country. A rocky mountain range separates the Land of Earth with the adjoining Land of Fire. These craggy peaks act as a natural fortress, protecting the Land of Fire from foreign incursions and shrouding it in mystery.

The Land of Fire is positioned in the center of the continent. Konohagakure, the village where Naruto was born and raised, is to be found here. Gently rolling hills spread throughout the land and, as most crops can be grown here, it is the most populous and bountiful of the countries. Because it lies in the center of the continent, it actively trades with the other countries, with many people coming and going. This has contributed to its economic development but also makes it an easy target for other countries. Because of this, it has put much effort into developing ninja, and from the past to the present, Konohagakure has turned out most of the best ninja.

The Land of Wind is located south of the Land of Earth and is home to the village of Sunagakure (lit. hidden among sand) where Gaara and his friends live. Though the country is huge, most of it is desert, and its population is therefore small. There is little rainfall, and the people live in settlements around oases dotted throughout the desert. Because the Land of Wind and the Land of Fire have an alliance, Sunagakure and Konohagakure appear to have an amicable relationship. However, the elder ninja of Sunagakure favor national defense over a military-reduction policy that promises to cut costs, leaving the village rippling with tension.

The Land of Water is the sole island nation among the Five Great Countries. The village of Kirigakure (lit. hidden among mist) is found here. It is surrounded by water on all four sides. Because of its unique mountainous geography, its population is small. There is little cultural exchange between the nearby smaller islands and each preserve their individual cultures.

There are hidden villages even in small nations outside the Five Great Ninja Countries. There is the village of Otokagakure (lit. hidden among sound) founded by Orochimaru, and the villages of Kusagakure (lit. hidden among grass), Ryuugakure (lit. hidden among waterfalls) and Amegakure (lit. hidden among rain), as well as others, that appear in the story.

See Keyword

Kumogakure
Raikage
Iwagakure
Tsuchikage
Konohagakure
Sunagakure
Gaara
Kirigakure
Otokagakure
Orochimaru
Kusagakure
Ryuugakure
Amegakure

See Question
03

03 What is the relationship between the states and their shinobi villages?

I t is said that the ninja villages came into existence when shinobi clans left the cities and moved to the mountains. At one time the world consisted of many small countries in a state of disarray, and the chaos of war was unceasing. But even during these times, due to the military might of the ninja, order was preserved, so ordinary people also moved into the hidden villages and they grew in size. When large nation states were eventually formed, the shinobi villages became part of them.

Each country is under the rule of a *daimyo,* or feudal ruler. Policy, such as distribution of the national budget to the villages, is set by the daimyo. The villages are administered by a chief. The ninja serve as the country's military force and are supported by the daimyo, who gives them the bulk of the country's budget. Because the main industry of a ninja village is the development of ninja, productivity is low and it is easy for such villages to fall into financial difficulty. Therefore, they have no choice but to be dependent on the national budget. However, because they contribute as the military force of the nation, they are rewarded with financial assistance from the state.

In the relationship between the state and the shinobi villages, the degree of favorable treatment received by the villages varies depending on the political policy of the daimyo. For example, because the Land of Fire lies in the center of the continent and is an easy target for other nations, the daimyo favors the ninja and provides them with a lot of financial help. In the Land of Wind, much of the territory is covered by desert and, by its very nature, it has a small national budget. The area along the border with the Land of Fire is mountainous, and the possibility of it being directly attacked is low. Because of this, the daimyo has instituted a military reduction policy, drastically cutting the budget for his country's ninja village Sunagakure, and follows a policy of hiring ninja from the Land of Fire in times of war. Because of these budget cuts, Sunagakure is weakening, and the ninja have a sense of crisis. Sunagakure's state of affairs is what is driving the push to artificially create "secret weapon" ninja, such as Gaara.

S **ee Keyword**

Sunagakure
Gaara

See Question
02

04 What was the Great Ninja World War?

The Great Ninja World War was the greatest war in history. The majority of the ninja villages scattered throughout the various lands participated and the whole world became a battlefield. The cause of the war was the power that the ninja had accrued from the daimyo. It was not a war caused by the clash of national politics, but a war in which ninja struggled for supremacy. Because it was not concentrated in one region, it developed into a struggle in which the entire world became a battlefield. It was fought based on the skill of ninja and, with this, heroes were created and new skills and techniques developed. On the other hand, because many lives were lost and because it became a war of attrition, the world was sapped of its strength.

05 How does someone become a ninja?

In order to become a ninja, one must enter the ninja academies the villages administer, study *jutsu* (techniques), and have one's skill verified by an instructor. Essentially, anyone can become a ninja. However, in reality, it is difficult to become a ninja unless one has special innate abilities, such as the possession of high *chakra* energy levels, or is born into a family line that boasts Kekkei Genkai (Bloodline Limit). Even if one doesn't have these inherent qualities, it is still possible to become a ninja through hard work, such as Rock Lee does.

With ninja techniques, there are various secrets particular to certain villages. Because of this, once a ninja graduates from a village academy, he must live his life in that village. Not only is becoming a ninja of another village forbidden, but leaving the village one belongs to is also not allowed. Ninja who break this rule and leave are known as *nukenin* (missing ninja). They are sometimes executed if discovered. This is in order to prevent jutsu developed by one village from being leaked to another. Some villages, such as Kirigakure, are particularly paranoid about this and have assigned special elite ninja as *oinin* (hunter ninja) for the purpose of hunting down and killing runaway ninja.

Konohagakure is, comparatively speaking, not that concerned about runaway ninja. There was little talk of going after Orochimaru when he left. The villagers have also made no effort to pursue and kill Uchiha Sasuke. This is because, as a topflight ninja, he is a necessary military force. Also, those who want him to return to the village have discovered his whereabouts and realize that there is little risk of him divulging his secrets. Konohagakure, which has many excellent ninja, appears to be lenient to runaways.

See Keyword

Kekkei Genkai
Rock Lee
Kirigakure
Konohagakure
Orochimaru
Sasuke

See Question
06 07

06 *What are a ninja's duties?*

The fundamental duty of a ninja is to fight as a soldier on the battlefield. Now that it is a time of peace, the ninja's principal daily duties include searching for lost children, working as bodyguards and arresting criminals. In this respect, they are not unlike policemen. They also work at the convenience of others, taking care of children, for example. Such duties are ordinarily assigned in the following manner. A member of the public puts in a request to a contact in the village. That contact determines the degree of difficulty of the request and assigns it a ranking of A to D. A corresponding service charge is set. The ninja leaders arrange these requests and allot each duty to the appropriate ninja.

The D-ranked duties are usually assigned to low-level ninja, or Genin (Low Ninja). However, no matter how simple a task may be, the ninja form a three-man team when they are called into action. This is because nothing is as important as teamwork to the ninja. The three-man team also allows novice ninja to learn how tasks are properly performed. Ordinary ninja called Jogi Butai perform these duties.

Konohagakure uses a system for B-level tasks deemed dangerous in which a ninja from a medical squad is attached to the three-man team to form a four-man group. It is a system encouraged by the Fifth Hokage Tsunade. Being a healing specialist, she regards nothing more important than the protection of ninja lives. The system is based on her belief that during the execution of dangerous missions, a healing ninja should always be on hand. Healing ninja train in a special unit where they learn how to use *chiyu* (healing) and *saisei* (revival) jutsu. In recent years, Konohagakure has put special emphasis on training such healing ninja.

In addition to the standard and healing squads, a special division known as Anbu has been established in Konohagakure. This division is directly under the control of the Hokage and performs secret tasks such assassinations, torture and monitoring of ninja to make sure there are no spies among them.

See Keyword

Konohagakure

See Question
05 07

07 *What are the ninja ranks?*

I n all ninja villages, the Kage (Shadow) occupies the highest rank. Immediately at his side is his advisory council, the Goikenban, and together they manage the affairs of the village's ninja. The Goikenban is mostly made up of former topflight ninja that have grown old and withdrawn from active service. They have a great deal of experience and give the Kage suitable advice at times when he is unsure about how to best formulate strategy. The Goikenban and the Kage together are known as *shunobu* (leaders).

The lowest ranked ninja are called Genin (Low Ninja). These are those who are just starting life as a ninja. If they do well in the Chunin trials and are recognized by high-ranked ninja, they advance to the rank of Chunin. Having become Chunin, they are recognized as proper ninja for the first time.

Chunin are selected from the Genin by means of trials. Chunin can act as leaders during the execution of tasks and teach at ninja academies.

Only ninja that excel can become Jonin (Elite Ninja). Jonin, such as Hatake Kakashi, Sarutobi Asuma and Might Guy, are often active as the heads of squads, commanders in battle, or leaders of Chunin and Genin. In addition, depending on the duties assigned to them, they can put together squads and combine their duties.

In the village of Konohagakure, there is a rank between Jonin and Chunin called Tokubetsu (Special) Jonin. Ninja of this rank often have special responsibilities. Examples of this incude Ebisu, who works as an exclusive tutor for Konohamaru; Kiba Inazuka's mother Tsume; and Genma Shiranui, Anko Mitarashi and Hayate Gekko, who act as judges at the Chunin trials.

See Keyword

Goikenban
Genin
Chunin
Jonin
Kakashi
Asuma
Might Guy
Tokubetsu Jonin
Ebisu
Konohamaru
Kiba
Genma Shiranui
Anko Mitarash

See Question
05 06

08 *What are nukenin and oinin?*

During the trials, ninja are initiated into secret skills specific to the villages to which they belong. If a ninja leaves his village, there is the risk that the village's secrets will be divulged. Therefore, leaving the village is ordinarily restricted unless there are orders. Also, even after they quit being ninja, they are not allowed to live outside the village. This is the fate of a ninja. Whoever joins this profession learns many top secrets and will inevitably learn the village's secret *ninjutsu*. If a ninja breaks this rule, he becomes a nukenin and will be hunted for the rest of his life.

It is impossible for each village to control the activities of every ninja. During battle, ninja will often try to persuade their opponents to turn traitor, although this is sometimes a trap. Because of such enticements, it is not rare for ninja to attempt to run away.

The mysterious group Akatsuki and the new village Otogakure are made up of runaway ninja.

Not only does the loss of a ninja result in the

weakening of the battle strength of a village, but if an absconding ninja becomes affiliated with another village, then that village can become a dangerous enemy. Also, because the unique *jujutsu* of the villages manifest themselves in the ninja's bodies, if a ninja is killed in battle it is not desirable for his corpse to fall into the hands of another village. The dead body of a ninja can be used in research by another village.

The village of Kirigakure has a special squad to assassinate runaway ninja. The Land of Water, home of Kirigakure, is the only island nation among the five great ninja countries, and much of it is mountainous. Because of these geographical conditions, it is not a prosperous country. Nevertheless, it is counted among the Five Great Ninja Countries because its ninja are secretive and have techniques that cannot be duplicated. This is because of Kirigakure's strictly-implemented *shosu seishin* (lit. few sharp minds) policy, by which ninja are forced to kill each other after graduating from the ninja academy.

Because of this policy, the ninja from Kirigakure are all top-level. If one runs away, the fighting strength of the village is weakened dramatically, while its weaknesses and secrets could become known by others. Runaways are a matter of life and death for the village. It therefore follows a policy of exhaustively hunting down and killing runaways. Oinin (hunter ninja) in their work as assassins are highly skilled at killing, and because they are even entrusted with the disposing of dead bodies, they are very good at healing jutsu as well.

See Keyword

Akatsuki
Otogakure
Kirigakure

09 *What kind of jutsu do the ninja use?*

The jutsu the ninja use are broadly divided into three types: taijutsu (body techniques), ninjutsu (ninja techniques), and genjutsu (illusion techniques).

Taijutsu such as *budo* (Japanese martial arts) and *kenpo* (the way of the hand) use the body to directly harm opponents. Rock Lee and Might Guy are the most skilled at using taijutsu. Of course, the users of taijutsu must become strong by training their bodies like a boxer and cultivating their power and speed. However, by controlling the chakra within them to make specific muscles superstrong, or by changing the very form of their bodies (such as with Choji's Baika (doubling) technique), they can increase their destructive powers.

Taijutsu that damage the nervous system and internal organs of an opponent through direct attacks are called juken (gentle fist). In order to effectively use *juken*, one must be able to see inside an opponent and view his nervous system or movement of his chakra. Unless one is born with a Kekkei Genkai (Bloodline Limit), such as Hyuga Neji, using juken is impossible.

Ninjutsu are the fundamental techniques in which most ninja specialize; there are a great variety of them and they entail such moves as changing the form of the refined chakra in one's body and striking an opponent with it, or converting the chakra into special energy and altering the form of one's body. There are quite a few different chakra, which vary depending on both the special nature of the village in which they originated and the unique nature of the ninja using them. Depending on the nature of the user's refined chakra, a ninja's techniques are divided into a number of jutsu, including Katon jutsu (Fire Release jutsu: turning chakra into fire and attacking) and Suiton jutsu (Water Release techniques: turning chakra into water and attacking).

Genjutsu disrupts the opponent's psychological state through hypnosis or by bringing on hallucinations. There are several types, such as aural genjutsu, which leads the target astray by creating special sounds, or visual genjutsu, such as the Sharingan (Copy Wheel Eye), which puts hallucinations in the minds of opponents. Also, *bunshin* (clone) jutsu can be said to be a type of genjutsu that uses illusions. Genjutsu are used on multiple targets at once, and although they have low physical attack power, by doing things like exhausting opponents and making them unable to move, they are very powerful as support jutsu.

Other than taijutsu, there are also jutsu such as *juin* (cursed seal) jutsu, used to place curses on opponents; *fuin* (sealing) jutsu, which use out-of-control chakra to seal up opponents; and *iryo* (medical) jutsu, used to heal injuries. There are indeed a great variety of techniques a ninja can use. On top of all this, there are also the techniques of a highly "top-secret" nature that only those who live in a certain area or belong to a certain clan can use; these are known as hidden (secret) techniques. Shikamaru's Kagemane (Shadow Imitation) jutsu or the Kikaichu (Destructive Bug Host) jutsu, which are only used by members of the Aburame clan, are examples of hidden jutsu that cannot be used by other ninja.

See Keyword

Taijutsu
Ninjutsu
Genjutsu
Rock Lee
Might Guy
Chakra
Choji
Juken
Kekkei Genkai
Sharingan
Juin
Shikamaru
Kikaichu

10 Why is the use of kinjutsu restricted?

There are ninjutsu that ninja are restricted from using. Among them are ninjutsu that overly expose their user to danger, such as Naruto's own specialty, the Kage Bunshin jutsu, or the Urarenge (Reverse Lotus) jutsu, which loosens the body's power controller and releases power greater than the body can handle. Other restricted techniques are ones that are so powerful it is impossible to imagine what would happen if they were used, or jutsu which violate the laws of nature, such as techniques which bring the dead back to life.

Naruto overuses the Kage Bunshin technique, which is a *kinjutsu*. It is an extraordinarily dangerous jutsu for the following reasons: as the clones it creates are all real matter, it uses a huge amount of chakra; in some situations the clones end up fighting among themselves; and the damage sustained by the individual clones accumulates as damage sustained by the user of the jutsu, and so, for example, if 10 clones sustain ten injuries then the user of the jutsu will sustain

100 wounds. It can be said that because Naruto is both able to use the immense amount of chakra carried by the Nine Tailed Demon Fox, and that he can have any injuries he sustains absorbed by the Demon Fox's chakra, then it is a technique especially suited to him.

The Edo Tensei (Impure World Resurrection) jutsu is said to bring the souls of the dead back into this world, but not only does it violate the laws of nature, but the revived corpses are not truly resurrected. If the user of the jutsu is killed, the spell cannot be undone. Returning a soul back to the world of the dead requires the use of the Shiki Fujin (Corpse Demon Seal Exhaustion) jutsu. This technique requires the user's soul to be exchanged for sealing away the soul of the dead. Therefore, a person's life is inevitably lost through the use of this jutsu.

See Keyword

Kage Bunshin
Urarenge
Edo Tensei
Shiki Fujin

11 What kinds of ningu exist?

See Keyword

Kankuro
Kiba Inuzuka
Akamaru

Ninja value nothing more than the ability to move freely, and fundamentally favor lightweight equipment. Throwing weapons, such as *makibishi* (caltrops), *shuriken* (throwing stars), and *kunai* (a type of ninja throwing knife) are the main components of their equipment. These don't have a lot of attack power, but they can impede an enemy's movements or strike from afar.

Most ninja carry tablets that provide nutrition and smoke bombs to blind their enemies. Cards, known as *kibakufuda* (explosive tags), with spells written on them that can cause explosions, and *makimono* (scrolls) that are read when one is summoning jutsu are carried by many ninja.

Some ninja carry special ningu in which they are specialized in handling. The puppets Kankuro uses in his Kugustu (Puppet) jutsu, Temari's giant fan, the demon brothers' kusarigama (sickle and chain), and Kiba Inuzuka's faithful *ninken* (ninja dog) companion Akamaru can all be viewed as ningu.

12 What is the chakra that gives the ninja his energy?

Chakra is a special energy source necessary for the use of ninjutsu. Using the life force that moves mind and body, and combinig it within the body, it allows the jutsu to be put into action when combined with seals. The quantity of life energy is called "stamina." Ninja can refine chakra as much as their stamina holds out, but, conversely, if they use chakra when their stamina is nearing zero, life energy is lost and the ninja will be paralyzed.

The amount of chakra consumed varies with the jutsu being brought into action. Being able to refine the right amount of chakra in their bodies to correspond with the jutsu being used is the hallmark of the truly excellent ninja. If chakra isn't efficiently created, stamina is used up wastefully.

For example, consider the ideal chakra use of Sakura Haruno. When she uses a skill that only requires 30 percent of her chakra, she makes 30 percent and retains 70 percent of her stamina.

The use of chakra by Sasuke Uchiha, on the

other hand, is wasteful. When he uses a technique that requires the same 30 percent of his chakra, he goes right ahead and makes 40 per cent, ultimately wasting 10 percent.

Naruto, for his part, even in times when refining 30 percent of chakra would suffice, ends up making 50 percent. Even worse, he is only able to put about 10 percent of his chakra to use whenever he uses ninjutsu, and so the original effect of those techniques is diluted. Sasuke and Naruto became skilled at the refinement of chakra during their training, but their clumsy technique when using jutsu causes them to waste life energy.

See Keyword

Chakra
Sakura
Sasuke Uchiha

See Question
13

13 *What are the chakra keitai henka and seishitsu henka?*

When ninja use the refined chakra in their body to put jutsu into action, *keitai henka* and *seishitsu henka* occur. Keitai henka is the term for the change of shape of chakra, such as the ball that is formed by the Rasengan (Spiraling Sphere), or the threads that form extending from his fingertips when Kankuro manipulates his puppets. The chakra spider webs that Kidomaru uses are another example of keitai henka. There are many ninja who change the shape of the refined chakra within them for use in jutsu, but these changes in shape are possibly precisely because chakra is energy.

Seishitsu henka is the term for the transformation of chakra (which was originally life energy) into physical matter when jutsu are used. In the Chidori (Thousand Birds) technique taught to Sasuke by Kakashi, the chakra energy's nature is changed into that of electrical energy and released. There are five types of seishitsu henka: earth, air, fire, water, and lightning. These basic nature are one of the origins of the names of the ninja countries, and are the basic principles behind all ninjutsu. The chakra made by ninja corresponds with one of these basic natures depending on the predisposition of the individual ninja. Because Sasuke's basic nature is that of fire, he specializes in Katon (Fire Release) jutsu. Provided they train, ninja are able to make chakra that does not correspond with their basic natures. Sasuke uses the lightning-based Chidori jutsu because he trained to change the nature of his chakra into lightning.

The basic ninjutsu are based on the five basic natures and are divided into the following: Katon, Futon, Suiton, Raiton, and Doton (respectively, Fire Release, Wind Release, Water Release, Lightning Release, and Earth Release). The jutsu the first Hokage devised is an extremely advanced technique through which he would simultaneously change the nature of his chakra into water and earth, instantaneously creating plant life by combining those two, and ultimately performing one technique after another using the essence of plants. Haku from the village of Kirigakure was also a user of special techniques he created by combining wind and water chakra to create the nature of ice. Ordinary ninja cannot combine different chakra like in those two examples. It is only possible for ninja who possess the special genetic abilities Kekkei Genkai.

See Keyword

Chakra
Rasengan
Kankuro
Kidomaru
Chidori
Sasuke
Kakashi
Haku
Kirigakure
Kekkei Genkai

See Question
12 14

35

14   *What are Kekkei Genkai?*

U nique physical abilities such as the Sharingan (Copy Wheel Eye) that are only apparent in certain people are known as Kekkei Genkai (Bloodline Limits). Those gifted with these qualities include members of the Uchiha clan, Kimimaro, who has the ability to make bones, and the Hyuga clan, who possess Byakugan (White Eye). Kekkei Genkai are special abilities that make use of genetic elements. The ability of Haku to use ice jutsu by simultaneously altering the natures of two types of chakra is also a Kekkei Genkai ability.

The special abilities that Kekkei Genkai enable are innate and cannot be acquired through training. The lines that carry the Kekkei Genkai, like the Hyuga and Uchiha clans, are often treated as nobility. However, there have been cases where whole families, such as Kirigakure's Haku family, have been murdered. There have been cases when someone, as in the case of Itachi Uchiha, is born into a Kekkei Genkai line and becomes so powerful and ambitious that he commits atrocities, such as killing his entire family or threatening the continued existence of his own village. Also, for the sake of the continued existence of the clan, there is a tendency to only value the main family. Because of this, branch families end up being sacrificed, as in the Hyuga clan's case. This gives rise to malcontents, such as Neji Hyuga, who have warped feelings about having been born into a branch clan.

Ninja that have Kekkei Genkai are promised great things. But such bloodlines can also turn out to be a curse.

See Keyword

Sharingan
Kekkei Genkai
Kimimaro
Kirigakure
Itachi Uchiha
Neji Hyuga

See Question
13

Chapter 02

Secrets of Naruto

15 What is the Nine Tailed Demon Fox sealed within Naruto?

The Nine Tailed Demon Fox that was sealed in Naruto's navel by the Fourth Hokage soon after he was born is one of what are known as tailed demons.

The tailed demons have anything from one to nine tails. Altogether nine of them exist. The One Tailed Shukaku that lives in Sunagakure's Gaara is another such tailed demon.

Fifteen years previous, during the early years of peace that followed the end of the Great Ninja World War, the Nine Tailed Demon Fox, which has the power to blast away mountains, suddenly attacked Naruto's village. It laid waste to the whole area and killed most of the villagers. The Fourth Hokage tried to fight off the Demon Fox and, using sealing jutsu, sacrificed his own life to seal the creature in Naruto's navel. Though it is sealed up, its spirit is still alive and its chakra can be continuously released to boost Naruto's jutsu. However, sometimes it releases evil energy that not even Naruto himself can control.

The tailed beasts possess unimaginable power.

There were ninja who contemplated using this power to their advantage during the Great Ninja World War. One of the methods devised was sealing the spirit of a tailed beast into a human, just as the Fourth Hokage sealed the Demon Fox into Naruto, and having that person use the power of the creature within. When Gaara was still in his mother's womb, the spirit of the Shukaku was actually within her. Gaara ended up becoming the host of the demon after he was born.

Gaara's unimaginable strength derives from the tailed beast Shukaku, and, in this same way, Naruto is able to display unbelievable strength through the power of the Demon Fox sealed inside him.

See Keyword

Nine Tailed Demon Fox
Hokage
Gaara

See Question

17

16 Who were Naruto's parents?

The Nine Tailed Demon Fox was sealed within Naruto's navel immediately after his birth to protect the village of Konohagakure, but it is not revealed in the story where Naruto's parents were at the time. Although it was for the sake of the village, it is difficult to imagine any parents capable of sacrificing their son in such a way. Therefore, it is believed that when Naruto became the container in which the Demon Fox was sealed, his parents were already dead.

Another possibility that can be considered is that Naruto is the son of the Fourth Hokage. The Fourth Hokage probably already knew how to seal away the Demon Fox before it appeared in the village. In other words, he was well aware of the necessity of using a newborn baby's body as a container. The Fourth Hokage sacrificed his own life to protect the village. A person willing to sacrifice his own life for the sake of others would probably be willing to give up his own son if it were necessary. Thus, there is every likelihood that the Fourth Hokage is Naruto's father.

The particulars of the Fourth Hokage's family makeup are not known. However, because Naruto was born after the village of Konohagakure came into being, his father was almost certainly a Konohagakure ninja. What we do know about the Hokage genealogy is as follows: the First and Second Hokage were brothers; the First Hokage's grandchild is the present Hokage Tsunade; the son of the Third Hokage is Asuma Sarutobi; and the Third Hokage's grandchild is Konohamaru. What is now unknown is who the descendents of the Second Hokage are. Those who succeed to the position of Hokage are all top-class ninja, so it is expected that those of the same bloodline are also highly-placed ninja. That is, there is a strong possibility that the Fourth Hokage is of the same bloodline as the First and Second Hokage. If Naruto is the son of the Fourth Hokage, then he too is part of that Hokage bloodline.

⑤ee Keyword

Nine Tailed Demon Fox
Fourth Hokage
Konohagakure
Third Hokage
Tsunade
Asuma Sarutobi

17 Why can't Naruto control the Demon Fox within him?

Though it is true that the Nine Tailed Demon Fox is sealed inside Naruto's body, it is nevertheless still alive and has a will of its own. That is, there exists a will within Naruto separate from his own. Also, because the Demon Fox does not currently have a body of its own, its spirit shares possession of Naruto's body. When Naruto sustains an injury at the hand of an enemy, the Demon Fox inside him also feels pain. In times of crisis, the form of the Demon Fox can be seen surrounding Naruto, while Naruto loses control completely. Ordinarily, Naruto moves his body as he wills it, but when Naruto is on the verge of death and his consciousness begins slipping away, the Demon Fox within him becomes mad with anger over the pain it also experiences. This rage is directed against the person who has caused this pain. The upshot of this is that Naruto loses control of his body to the Demon Fox and goes on a rampage.

Fifteen years have already passed since the Demon Fox was sealed inside Naruto. The seal that the Fourth Hokage sacrificed his life to place has weakened with the passage of time. On the occasions when the form of the Demon Fox appears around Naruto, it seems that if four or more tails are visible then Naruto loses control over his body. The only person in Konohagakure who is skilled in the jutsu that the Hokage used to seal away the Nine Tailed Demon Fox is Yamato, who carries the DNA of the First Hokage.

See Keyword

Nine Tailed Demon Fox
Fourth Hokage
Yamato

See Question
15

18 *Is Naruto a human weapon?*

Born in the village of Sunagakure, Gaara came into the world as a human weapon by the leaders of the village. Since such newly-borns can use the power of the tailed beasts sealed within them, there is every chance that they will grow up to be extraordinarily powerful ninja. Villages with such ninja can dominate, with such ninja becoming a kind of secret weapon. As for Gaara, he came into this world as a kind of artificial life form when the Shukaku already sealed within a teapot was taken and combined with him while he was still inside his mother's womb.

Naruto, on the other hand, had the Nine Tailed Demon Fox sealed within him when it attacked the village, and there was no other course of action for the Fourth Hokage. However, when Jiraiya inspected the seal on Naruto, he discovered that the seal was written so that the great chakra of the Demon Fox could be used by Naruto. Before he met Jiraiya, Naruto was not aware of this power, because Orochimaru had placed a new seal over the one given by the Fourth Hokage. Jiraiya removed Orochimaru's seal, enabling Naruto to utilize the Demon Fox's chakra and benefit from high level jutsu, such as Rasengan.

With this in mind, we can speculate that the Fourth Hokage's plans were to turn Naruto into a human weapon. If one considers that the Demon Fox's counterpart, the Shukaku, was sealed in a teapot, it becomes clear that the Demon Fox could have been sealed in another container, and not within Naruto. This adds credence to the belief that the Fourth Hokage deliberately sealed the Demon Fox inside Naruto to make him a human weapon. Also, if Gaara is the biological son of the previous Kazekage, then it seems all the more possible that Naruto is of the Hokage bloodline.

See Keyword

Sunagakure
Gaara
Shukaku
Nine Tailed Demon Fox
Rasengan
Kazekage

19 Is Naruto safe using the kinjutsu Kage Bunshin?

T he first powerful jutsu Naruto learned was the kinjutsu Kage Bunshin (Shadow Clone). The ordinary Bunshin technique is a type of genjutsu, and though it looks like there are many clones, only the source of the clones is real. In contrast to this, the Kage Bunshin clones are real matter, and it is a powerful technique through which an enemy can be directly attacked.

It is restricted because an enormous amount of chakra is required to bring the jutsu into action, and since the clones are real matter, the damage they sustain accumulates in the user of the jutsu. This makes it an extremely dangerous technique. However, Naruto inevitably uses it whenever he does battle, although it never appears to harm him. Naruto has the Demon Fox inside him, and has the special ability of being able to quickly recover even from injuries that bring him to the brink of death thanks to the Demon Fox and the strength of its chakra. That is, using the Demon Fox's chakra, he is an extraordinarily strong ninja when it comes to sustaining injuries, and even overuse of the Kage Bunshin does no expose him to danger. This is an ability very few normal people have. In this way, the Kage Bunshin is an extremely powerful jutsu for Naruto, and it shouldn't really be restricted.

See Keyword

Kage Bunshin
Nine Tailed Demon Fox
Chakra

See Question
10

20 Why is Naruto able to quickly recover from his wounds?

We all know that Naruto is able to recover surprisingly quickly even from injuries that put him at death's door. He can recover from fatigue very quickly as well. This ability is not inborn, but derives from the power of the Demon Fox sealed within him.

The Demon Fox is a spirit without a body, and so it shares Naruto's body with him. When Naruto is hurt, the Demon Fox sustains the injury as well. The Demon Fox uses its special powers to heal itself, and effectively heals Naruto in the process. That is, Naruto has not only been granted the Demon Fox's great chakra, but also receives the blessings of the Demon Fox when he is injured. Naruto is aware of the spirit of the fox within him, and sometimes is able to have it divide up chakra for him. Naruto consciously conducts this apportioning of chakra, but when he benefits from the healing power of the Demon Fox it is an unconscious process. Like Rock Lee, Naruto often pushes his body to perform beyond its limitations because of his strong spirit. Thanks to the healing power of the Demon Fox, even if he pushes himself beyond its limits and goes too far, he quickly recovers.

🇸ee Keyword

Nine Tailed Demon Fox
Rock Lee

21 What kind of jutsu is Naruto's specialty, the Rasengan?

The Rasengan is a jutsu originally developed by the Fourth Hokage, who of course learned it from the Rasengan master, Jiraiya. Jiraiya probably taught it to Naruto because, though Naruto is a slow jutsu learner, he and Jiraiya are similar.

Huge amounts of chakra are put into the Rasengan, which forms a ball in the hand. The chakra on the palm of the hand revolves until it becomes something akin to having a typhoon in one's hand. This chakra isn't thrown at enemies, but rather strikes them and pushes them down. In other words, it is a direct attack, and that is what probably makes Naruto suited for it. The spinning ball of chakra has devastating power, and opponents struck by it are ripped apart.

The Rasengan has another strong point — it is simple to use in spite of its power. Lots of chakra is put into it, and if the user manages to make it spin, it can be put into action without the need for a Seishitsu Henka. Even an impatient klutz like Naruto doesn't screw it up once he learns the basics behind the technique. It has gained prominence precisely because it is used by Naruto and his ability to call forth the chakra of the Demon Fox.

When he was learning this jutsu, the clumsy Naruto used the Kage Bunshin and cooperated with the clones to perfect the jutsu. Because the clones themselves were also able to channel chakra into one point, it created an even more powerful Rasengan. Naruto is usually full of ideas for the use of the Kage Bunshin. He is quite good at using the clones as decoys to outsmart his opponents and betray their expectations or throw them into disarray. Being this sort of ideas man also comes in handy when putting the Rasengan into action.

ⓢee Keyword

Nine Tailed Demon Fox
Rasengan

22 Why is Naruto taking on the form of the fox more and more?

Rampages by the Demon Fox sealed within Naruto have in recent years become more frequent. In the past, only when Naruto sustained injuries that brought him to the edge of death, the malevolent spirit of the Demon Fox would manifest itself around him. Recently, however, even at times when Naruto gets excited during training, malefic chakra assumes the form of the Demon Fox. It is said that if four or more tails appear then there is a chance that the seal will be broken.

It is believed that this is because the sealing jutsu placed by the Fourth Hokage is weakening, but it also seems that Naruto's use of the Demon Fox is another reason. Back when Naruto first became aware of the Demon Fox sealed within him, his spirit and the Demon Fox's were unable to get along and he could not use its power even if he tried. But he has gradually come to understand how to channel the Demon Fox's energy. As long as it is firmly sealed away, the Demon Fox can't wield that power. So it seems that Naruto through his own volition is setting the spirit of the Demon Fox within him free so that if things get out of hand, it will take over his body.

ee Keyword

Nine Tailed Demon Fox
Fouth Hokage

See Question
17

23 How did Kakashi recruit Naruto?

Learning new ninjutsu isn't Naruto's strong point, but he does have his one great skill, the Rasengan. The Fourth Hokage developed it further, but it is not yet perfect. The Rasengan, which is chakra transformed into a ball on the palm of the hand, is used to strike an opponent. If a Seishitsu Henka is applied to this, then it can become an even more destructive jutsu. The Fourth Hokage seems to originally have had the idea of applying a Seishitsu Henka to the Rasengan.

Some ninja are good at applying Seishitsu Henka to chakra and some are not. There are ninja who are good at changing chakra into fire and there are ninja who are good at changing chakra into wind, so it is necessary for ninja to independently research and develop such techniques, as learning them from a teacher is impossible. Therefore, in the creation of jutsu that entail applying chakra to the Rasengan, Naruto has to develop them himself. However, because mastering ninjutsu is not Naruto's forte, he isn't very good at Seishitsu Henka.

Kakashi has taught Naruto how to increase the power of his Rasengan and develop new ninjutsu himself. However, the ability of the Kage Bunshin clones to all do the same thing was what Kakashi used to entice and recruit Naruto. The Kage Bunshin is not a genjutsu, and so the clones created by it are real. Also, the user of the jutsu receives feedback from the actions of the clones. The Kage Bunshin is a kinjutsu because the damage the clones sustain feeds back to its user. However, its special trait can be put to use during training. For example, if ten clones are created and the clones do the same thing, then it is as if the user of the jutsu had done the same thing ten times.

Kakashi made Naruto learn the Kage Bunshin first and had him use clones to practice Seishitsu Henka. Using this method, Naruto would be able to cover a lot of ground in a surprisingly short amount of time and quickly learn the basics of Seishitsu Henka.

This method of training requires an immense amount of chakra. The clones created by the Kage Bunshin technique (which itself eats up a lot of chakra) also consume a lot chakra individually. This method can only be used by Naruto due to his access to the Demon Fox's chakra. With this training, Naruto perfects the Futon Rasen Shuriken (Wind Release: Spiral Shuriken) in a spectacularly short amount of time.

See Keyword

Rasengan
Kakashi
Chakra
Kage Bunshin
Futon Rasen Shuriken

See Question
13 **24**

24 What kind of jutsu is the Rasen Shuriken?

See Keyword

Rasen Shuriken
Rasengan

See Question
23

The Rasen Shuriken (Spiral Shuriken) created by Kakashi is a Rasengan that has had its nature changed to that of wind. In a manner of speaking it is a "revised edition" of the Rasengan.

The Rasengan is a ball of chakra that is compressed into the palm of the hand and used to strike an opponent. When it spins and strikes the enemy it has considerable destructive power due to its compressed chakra energy. The Rasen Shuriken undergoes an elemental recomposition into the same "wind" nature as Naruto, and the spinning chakra transforms into the shape of a shuriken (throwing star). The chakra becomes like an infinite number of needles, and has an effect like poison as it destroys the cells of an opponent one by one. However, it has a defect—the needles of the shuriken can pierce the cells of Naruto's palm to harm him too. It is likely that if Naruto continuously uses this technique, the palms of his hands will be ground into hamburger

25 Will Naruto die if the spirit of the Demon Fox escapes from him?

Those who have tailed beasts sealed within them are called *jinchuriki*. Jinchuriki were created by researchers during the Great Ninja World War for the purpose of developing even more powerful ninja. After the war, to make the weakened village of Sunagakure more powerful, Gaara was made into a monster using the one-tailed beast Shukaku. Jinchuriki make the fearsome and mysterious powers of the tailed beasts their own and use them to become very powerful ninja. However, if the tailed beast's spirit is lost, the jinchuriki die.

Naruto is not a jinchuriki; Fourth Hokage had no one else in which to seal the Nine Tailed Demon Fox when it suddenly attacked Konohagakure. Nevertheless, Naruto is a container for a tailed beast and, like the jinchuriki, he will die if the spirit of the beast inside him slips away. That is, Naruto cannot live the life of a normal human being; he is fated to spend his life trying to coexist with the Demon Fox.

See Keyword

Nine Tailed Demon Fox

See Question
18

Chapter 03

Secrets of the Ninja from Konohagakure

26 When was Konohagakure founded?

The village Konohagakure came into being about 60 years prior to the current story arc. A great ninja who later became the First Hokage gathered other ninja in a quiet forest clearing far from any urban center, and the village began to take shape. The ninja lived together in the forest and built houses. As the world fell into chaos, these ninja became active in the growing conflict, and other noted ninja also joined them in the forest. The collective grew, and more people began doing work, such as hunting and fishing, outside the scope of ninja duties. Eventually the settlement developed into a village. The village was formally named Konohagakure, and its leader took the title of Hokage.

The daimyo of the Land of Fire viewed Konohagakure as the source of his military might, and the village received much financial assistance. The upshot of this was that many people who were not ninja began to turn up at the gates of Konohagakure, and the village developed into the place it is today.

Konohagakure became the Land of Fire's military center. The Great Ninja World War broke out. Eventually, as a result of alliances formed between the different states, peace was achieved. However, Konohagakure still receives favorable treatment from the Land of Fire as a place where elite ninja are trained as a police-like force that protects the country.

See Keyword

Konohagakure
Hokage

See Question
27

27 Who were the past Hokage?

The First Hokage was the founder of Konohagakure. By simultaneously channeling water and earth chakra, and then combining them, he was able to use the special Mokuton (Wood Release) jutsu. Therefore he had a special inborn ability not unlike a Kekkei Genkai. He probably gave the village he created a wood-related name (Konohagakure literally means "hidden in the woods") because he was the user of this Wood Release technique. He most likely took a fire-related title (Hokage literally means "fire shadow") because he was from the Land of Fire.

However, the village was founded during a tumultuous period. The First Hokage spent much of his time on the battlefield, fighting for his country, and he was killed before he could fully implement his plans for the village.

The Second Hokage contributed greatly to the development of the village left incomplete by his brother, the First Hokage. The ninja became organized under his reign. He founded the ninja academy, and created much of the system used to raise master ninja. However, during his reign, the Great Ninja World War broke out, and, like his brother, he fell in battle.

After the death of the Second Hokage, his pupil Sarutobi took the helm. The name "Sarutobi" is that of a line of great Japanese ninja. This Sarutobi was not a relative of the First and Second Hokage; it was his excellence as a ninja that enabled his succession. He was nicknamed "Professor" as he was quite accomplished in researching ninjutsu; he discovered most of the ninjutsu used in Konohagakure. His reign was after the end of the Great Ninja World War, and to keep the chaos of war from returning, he began negotiating with the Kage (the heads of other villages). By keeping his mind on the balance of military power to prevent the world from returning to conflict, and by teaching the ninja of Konohagakure the importance of protecting their comrades, he made many contributions to the cause of peace. While still alive, he relinquished his title of Hokage to his young grandchild and pupil, and retired.

However, the Fourth Hokage lost his life in the attack of the Nine Tailed Demon Fox, and once again Sarutobi took over.

Strictly speaking, he was both Third and the Fifth Hokage, and spent more years in power than anyone else. When Sarutobi's former pupil and acolyte Orochimaru tried to destroy Konohagakure in a coup d'état, Sarutobi retaliated. Orochimaru reanimated the First and Second Hokage with his kinjutsu Edo Tensei (Impure World Resurrection). Sarutobi had to sacrifice his own life when he used the Shiki Fujin (Corpse Demon Seal Exhaustion) jutsu to send their spirits back to the world of the dead.

⑤ee Keyword

The First Hokage
Kekkei Genkai
The Second Hokage
Konohagakure
Fourth Hokage
Nine Tailed Demon Fox
Orochimaru
Edo Tensei
Shiki Fujin

See Question
26

28 What kind of person is the current Hokage, Tsunade?

The fifth and current Hokage, Tsunade, is the granddaughter of the first. She is one of the three legendary ninja (along with Jiraiya and Orochimaru), and was the pupil of the Third Hokage. After the fall of the Third Hokage, the Goikenban recommended Jiraiya as the next Hokage. However, Jiraiya withdrew himself from consideration and recommended Tsunade in his place.

Tsunade isn't just an excellent ninja; the effects of the teaching of the third Hokage are strongly apparent in her. Because of this, she is a ninja who values nothing more than life and is adept at healing jutsu. Jiraiya was aware of his own hot-blooded nature and probably felt that the life-valuing Tsunade was more appropriate for the job. She is also right for the role because she is the First Hokage's grandchild and part of the Hokage bloodline.

In the time of the Great Ninja World War, Tsunade lost both her lover and her little brother on the battlefield, and was traumatized by the horrific bloodshed. She began to have doubts about the life of a ninja and left the village. But she realized her own significance lay in using the healing jutsu she was pursuing; even on her own she could save the lives of many ninja, and so resolved to become the next Hokage. Since becoming leader, Tsunade has invested in training healing ninja. In previous times, it was customary for the ninja teams to have only three members. However, she implemented a system by which each team also includes a healing ninja.

It is said that the mortality rate for ninja in Konohagakure has markedly decreased since Tsunade took over. She also has extraordinary mystical power, and can create a fissure in the ground with one punch.

Rumor has it that when she was young, she caught Jiraiya peaking into a women's bathhouse and beat him so badly that she nearly killed him.

See Keyword

Tsunade
Jiraiya
Orochimaru
Third Hokage
Goikenban

See Question
27 29

The three legendary ninja are Jiraiya, Tsunade, and Orochimaru. All three were pupils of the Third Hokage, but they weren't just outstanding ninja; they also excelled at summoning jutsu. Orochimaru summons snake monsters, Jiraiya summons frog monsters, and Tsunade summons slugs. Snakes are weak against slugs, slugs are weak against frogs, and frogs are weak against snakes. Because of this, when the three of them fight at the same time, there is a perfect balance of power; no one can gain the upper hand and the fight is never settled.

As students of the Third Hokage, the trio once performed duties as a three-man team similar to that of Naruto, Sasuke and Sakura. However, Orochimaru had ambitions about moving up in the world. His ambition got too strong and, to become powerful, he started researching the Furo Fushi (Immortality) kinjutsu. Because of this, he was unable to become the Fourth Hokage and left the village.

Jiraiya, for his part, is an individualist who loves solitude. He considered a way of life in which he would have to dedicate himself to the village undesirable, and left to become an itinerant.

Tsunade is the granddaughter of the First Hokage and loves Konohagakure. However, due to her trauma after losing both her little brother and lover to war, she left to wander outside the village.

Because of these events, the young ninja of Naruto's generation went a long time without ever seeing the three legendary ninja. They were designated "legendary" ninja because no one knew anything of them other than what they had heard from legends.

Tsunade is currently the Fifth Hokage; her friend Jiraiya helps her out in ways similar to the Goikenban, and together they take care of the village.

Orochimaru was killed by Sasuke in the middle of the second series of the saga, but because he was researching the Furo Fushi, it's possible that he could come back to life.

See Keyword

Tsunade
Jiraiya
Orochimaru
Sasuke
Sakura
Third Hokage
First Hokage
Konohagakure
Goikenban

After founding Otogakure, Orochimaru brought his ninja to Konohagakure under the pretext of having them participate in the Chunin trials. He assassinated the head of Sunagakure (the Kazekage), assumed his form, and got the ninja of Sunagakure to also participate in an attempted coup d'état. The coup ended in failure and Konohagakure eluded destruction, but the Third Hokage had to sacrifice his life.

Though the coup d'état itself ended in failure, Orochimaru didn't actively do anything to destroy Konohagakure. The coup attempt wasn't so he could become the new Hokage. He felt that he was the greatest of ninja, but did not receive his due recognition. Therefore, he hated both the Third Hokage (who passed him over for promotion to the Fourth Hokage), and Konohagakure itself. In truth, the Third Hokage recognized Orochimaru as the most powerful ninja, but because Orochimaru studied kinjutsu to make himself even stronger, the Hokage felt that

Orochimaru had only selfish interests. He decided he could not entrust Orochimaru with the role of Hokage, and did not select him as his successor. In other words, Orochimaru just wasn't cut out to be a Hokage. However, Orochimaru is indeed powerful and sees value in nothing but strength. By attacking the village of Konohagakure, he sought to show just how powerful he really was.

Orochimaru, unlike the third Hokage, wasn't the type of guy to sacrifice his life to protect a village, but the Third Hokage showed Orochimaru that willingness to sacrifice one's life was the calling card of a true Hokage. Strictly viewed as a matter of life and death, Orochimaru "won" the battle with the Third Hokage. Viewed from the perspective of how a life should be lived, however, the actions of the Third Hokage are more impressive. One has to wonder if Orochimaru at the very least felt anything in the face of the Third Hokage's self-sacrificing and magnanimous attitude.

Since the failed coup, there is still friction between Orochimaru and Konohagakure, but these are due to his feud with Sasuke, and not because of any hair-splitting over who is the strongest. Orochimaru now has little interest in Konohagakure.

See Keyword

Orochimaru
Konohagakure
Sunagakure
Kazekage
Third Hokage

See Question
29 31

31 What is Orochimaru plotting now?

Orochimaru founded Otogakure and attempted the coup with the aim of destroying Konohagakure. For a while he seems to have been a member of Akatsuki, but later apparently worked independently in Otogakure. He had bases throughout the world, where he kept captives who seemed to be engaged in some kind of research. Why did he have bases and what was he researching?

Orochimaru knows how to use jutsu to possess the bodies of others and be liberated from the aging process by always having a young body. When the body he takes over ages, it becomes necessary for him to find a new one. He wants to remain a strong ninja even after each "rebirth," so he thinks that the best candidates for possession are other powerful ninja. At first he wanted Kimimaro from the Kaguya clan to be his next host body, but Kimimaro fell ill with an incurable disease and if Orochimaru took over his body, Orochimaru would have soon died. He hurriedly selected the body of Sasuke Uchiha as the next candidate. The time for changing to the next body was imminent but he couldn't get his hands on Sasuke. He then decided he had no choice but to make the men imprisoned in his bases fight to the death, and took over the body of the last man standing. He is unable to move to the next host body until three years have passed using the current one; if he did manage to move into Sasuke's body, it would be three years later at the earliest. Orochimaru put a special cursed seal on Sasuke and made him more powerful. Since Sasuke is only interested in power, he headed for Orochimaru's base and began to work with him.

In the following three years, to develop Sasuke into his next host body, Orochimaru had Sasuke train in various ways and gave him special jutsu. Sasuke can now sprout wings from his back and is no longer really human. Orochimaru seems to have conducted experiments on live people for the ultimate goal of creating a superhuman like Sasuke. Orochimaru was interested in nothing besides taking over Sasuke's body, and it's not at all clear what he intended to do after achieving this goal.

Orochimaru tried to take over Sasuke's body, but failed miserably and was killed by Sasuke. Orochimaru had immortality and no one really knows if he truly was killed, but his failure to take over Sasuke's body is not in doubt.

See Keyword

Orochimaru
Otogakure
Konohagakure
Akatsuki
Kimimaro
Sasuke Uchih

See Question
30

32 Why did Itachi Uchiha massacre his clan?

The Uchiha clan has the Sharingan (Copy Wheel Eye) Kekkei Genkai, and is one of the noteworthy clans (along with the Hyuga clan and their Byakugan (White Eye) Kekkei Genkai. Most members of the Uchiha clan are in high positions in Konohagakure. Since very young, Itachi displayed great talent and was referred to as the pride of the Uchiha clan. Itachi himself began to hate it when he saw that his own special powers were seen as stemming from his being part of the Uchiha line. Itachi really was a great ninja, but many great ninja have a bad habit of seeing themselves as superior. As Itachi developed, he became even stronger, and, like Orochimaru, his megalomania worsened by the day.

When he was assigned to Anbu, he undertook top secret work, while developing a tendency to look down on his village and his clan. To become more powerful, he had to become more heartless, and became intolerable of the things to which he was bound, such as village and clan. His assassination of his closest friend Hisui Uchiha, who had adored him like an older brother, to get the Mangekyo Sharingan (Kaleidoscope Copy Wheel Eye, more powerful than the Sharingan) serves as proof of this. Ultimately, on the night of a full moon, he massacred almost the entire Uchiha clan, and then fled the village.

Itachi even today wears a headband identifying him as a ninja of Konohagakure, but the marking of "Konoha" is badly defaced. The meaning of this is that he has cut his ties to the village.

See Keyword

Itachi Uchiha
Sharingan
Kekkei Genkai
Konohagakure
Mangekyo Sharingan

See Question
33

33 Why did Itachi join Akatsuki?

See Keyword
Itachi Uchiha
Akatsuki
Konohagakure
Nine Tailed Demon Fox

See Question
32 67 68

As a member of the mysterious organization Akatsuki, Itachi often appears around Konohagakure during his attempts to get hold of the Nine Tailed Demon Fox sealed within Naruto. Itachi is wanted for butchering his clan, and is a nukenin, so why does he feel he has to take such a risk by coming to Konohagakure?

In truth, at this point in time no one knows what Itachi's real reason was for joining Akatsuki. Akatsuki is plotting world conquest, but looking at Itachi's past actions, it is difficult to believe that he joined Akatsuki because he endorses the goals of its members and wants to help them. Right now he seems to be helping them, but that is probably because he sees this as a quick route to whatever it is he really wants to accomplish.

34 Why is Sasuke Uchiha so caught up in becoming powerful?

The best ninja in Naruto's class at the academy was Sasuke. Nevertheless, he still wanted to become stronger. This wasn't because he aspired to be a powerful ninja. He hates his older brother Itachi (who robbed Sasuke of his family by massacring the whole clan) from the bottom of his heart and has made killing Itachi his life's goal. Sasuke fully understands that Itachi is a much stronger ninja than himself, and that he once respected and looked up to him. Thus, he must become a stronger ninja than Itachi, and aspires to become the most powerful ninja in the world. Sasuke is cognizant of the fact that the power he derives from the cursed seal placed on him by Orochimaru is evil. Nonetheless, he feels that he must find a way to become powerful, and ends up becoming a follower of Orochimaru. Like Itachi and Orochimaru before him, Sasuke has become a ninja with no interest in anything but power; his desire to destroy Itachi made him that way.

See Keyword

Sasuke Uchiha
Itachi Uchiha
Orochimaru

See Question
32 35

35 Why did Sasuke Uchiha leave his village?

When Orochimaru chose Sasuke as the next person to host his soul, he ordered him to become one of the Sound Four. The lives of the Sound Four were in the control of Orochimaru (i.e., he set it up so he could kill them whenever he felt like it). However, they possessed superhuman strength. As one of them, Sasuke also had a cursed seal on him, and eventually he began to desire the superhuman power of it, and did things like take the *kakuseigan* (stimulant pills)—medicine used to make his cursed seal advance to level 2 more rapidly.

Naruto and the others set out to rescue Sasuke, but ultimately Sasuke ignores Naruto and, of his own volition, chooses to remain under Orochimaru. This is not only because Sasuke is taken with the power of Orochimaru's cursed seal. He believes friendships and ties with the village make him weak, and therefore he must cut himself off if he wants to achieve the power he seeks. Sasuke turned his back on his friends and left the village because he felt it was necessary for him to become stronger.

Sasuke is now being pursued as a nukenin. The Sasuke known to Kakashi and the others is the old Sasuke, the one not obsessed with power. The villagers know that the slaughter of his family and clan is what made Sasuke heartless. They don't treat him as dangerous, but instead search for him and pray for his return.

See Keyword

Sasuke Uchiha
Orochimaru
Kakuseigan
Kakashi

See Question
32 **35**

82

36 *Why does Sasuke have wings?*

Having spent three years at Orochimaru's base, Sasuke acquired a superhuman form, with bat-like wings growing from his back.

It is obvious that the spider-like form of Sasuke's fellow Sound Four member Kidomaru is another example of the same phenomenon that produced Sasuke's wings. However, it is not known if these were the result of the seals or the experiments Orochimaru was conducting on live humans.

Orochimaru's cursed seals bestow unimaginable powers. The changes in form, like Orochimaru's own transformation into something snake-like, were probably the result of Orochimaru's research into using jutsu to combine humans with animals. Sasuke was perhaps the one great success of these experiments. Combining the power of the seals with this research, Orochimaru was probably trying to create super-humans similar to the jinchuriki. In all likelihood, he temporarily became a member of Akatsuki because the group carries out research on the jinchuriki. It is thought that after getting his hands on whatever he was after, being a member became no longer necessary, and he left. Also, Sasuke is believed to have volunteered to become the subject of Orochimaru's research in order to acquire overwhelming power. Of course, Orochimaru didn't give Sasuke these powers for Sasuke's sake, but did it for self-serving reasons as he planned to take over Sasuke's body next.

Ⓢee Keyword

Sasuke Uchiha
Orochimaru
Kidomaru
Jinchuriki
Akatsuki

37 Did Sasuke kill Orochimaru?

When attempting to take over Sasuke's body, Orochimaru forced his way into his mind and tried to chase out his spirit. However, within Sasuke's mind, Orochimaru fell victim to the Sharingan. Orochimaru's own genjutsu were used against him, dragging him into the world of illusion he himself created, and the attempted takeover failed. After his spirit slipped out of Sasuke, Orochimaru was killed when Sasuke sliced and diced his giant snake form into pieces.

However, after killing Orochimaru, Sasuke has strange experiences in which he turns into a giant snake. He also names the team he leads Hebi, or "snake." These actions make one wonder if he hasn't become Orochimaru.

Also, Orochimaru's faithful underling Kabuto Yakushi put some of the fallen Orochimaru's cells into his own body. Because of this, part of his body changes into a snake-like form and he has become a snake-man just like Orochimaru.

Orochimaru may very well still be alive, his

mind and body split—the former now in Sasuke and the latter in Kabuto Yakushi.

See Keyword

Sasuke Uchiha
Orochimaru
Sharingan
Kabuto Yakushi

38 Who are the members of the four-man Hebi group formed by Sasuke?

After leaving the base following his killing of Orochimaru, Sasuke recruited a group from Orochimaru's other bases. Together with his cohorts (Karin, Jugo and Suigetsu), he formed the four-man group he dubbed Hebi (meaning "snake").

Suigetsu, one of the Hozuki Brothers, is a ninja from Kirigakure. He is cruel, and playfully kills his opponents bit by bit by chopping of their hands and feet, rendering them immobile. Because of this, he is said to be the second coming of Zabuza. Suigetsu himself reveres Zabuza, and can wield Zabuza's *kubikiri* (a knife used by samurai for decapitation).

(It's said that the ninja of Kirigakure have a system through which they hand down swords through generations, and that a ninja's sword may only be used by his successor. Suigetsu was intended to be the successor of Zabuza, and can use the kubikiri that only Zabuza used.)

The next in the group, Karin, was once an underling of Orochimaru and watched over the prisoners kept at his bases. She has a thing for Sasuke and is totally smitten when they are alone together. However, if caught with him, her demeanor changes entirely, and she acts as if she has no interest in Sasuke whatsoever. She also has a knack for tracking down people.

The next, Jugo has also been given a cursed seal by Orochimaru and can change the form of his body whenever the mood strikes. He has two personalities—normally a nice guy, an uncontrollably savage character takes over when he gets the urge to kill. He is on close terms with Kimimaro, who is the only person to whom he has shown any mercy.

The three have so little regard for one another that there is effectively no teamwork between them. But Sasuke believes the trio to be essential to his plans to destroy Itachi, whom they hunt as the group Hebi.

See Keyword

Sasuke Uchiha
Orochimaru
Hebi
Karin
Jugo
Suigetsu
Kirigakure
Zabuza
Kimimaro

39 Why does Tsunade go after Itachi?

See Keyword

Tsunade
Itachi Uchiha
Konohagakure
Akatsuki
Sasuke Uchiha
Orochimaru
Kakashi

A long time has passed since Itachi fled Konohagakure. And although his name is on the list of those wanted for the slaughter of his family, Tsunade has hesitated to give orders for his capture. It is quite possible that she believed that such a mission is fraught with danger, given Itachi's power.

Konohagakure's greatest challenge is the hunt for Akatsuki in order to destroy it. However, Jiraiya brings news that Sasuke has killed Orochimaru and escaped. She realizes that Sasuke is now going after Itachi, and wherever Itachi goes, Sasuke is sure to follow.

Furthermore, because Itachi is a member of Akatsuki, she is able to combine the hunt for him with the hunt for the organization. With Kakashi in charge, an eight-member team that includes Naruto, Yamato, Hina, Kiba, Shino, Sakura and Sai sets off to track down Itachi.

40 Why is Kakashi able to use the Sharingan?

Of the Konohagakure ninja, Kakashi is either top or a close second. He is the son of Sakumo Hatake, the famous ninja nicknamed the White Fang of Konoha.

Kakashi displayed remarkable ninja talent when young, but since acquiring the Sharingan, he has used the Copy Wheel Eye to acquire any ninjutsu he fancies. Because of this, he has been dubbed a "copy ninja," and it's thought that there are almost no ninjutsu he isn't capable of.

The Sharingan was originally a Kekkei Genkai possessed only by members of the Uchiha clan. There was no reason to expect someone outside the clan, such as Kakashi, to be able to use it. Kakashi's Sharingan came, in fact, from his close friend, Obito Uchiha.

During the fight at Kannabi Bridge, Kakashi's failure to put the lives of his friends first resulted in the death of his close friend, Obito. Kakashi believed that a ninja's execution of duty was paramount. Obito revealed how different his own feelings were during the rescue of their friend

Rin when he mocked those that don't value their friends above all else. The two ended up failing to work together as a team on the battlefield.

Kakashi eventually realizes the importance of friends and begins following Obito's example. But during the rescue of Rin, Kakashi loses his left eye in a fight and Obito is mortally wounded. He manages one last wish, beseeching Kakashi to "take my eye." With the help of the ninja medic Rin, Obito's left eye is removed and inserted into the empty socket in Kakashi's face. Henceforth, Kakashi has the Sharingan ability in his left eye.

Obito's eye has allowed the highly talented Kakashi to move up to the next ninja level, making him the master he is today.

Ⓢee Keyword

Kakashi
Sharingan
Konohagakure
Kekkei Genkai
Obito Uchiha
Rin

41 What is the Kikaichu jutsu?

The unique ninjutsu Kikaichu (Destruction Bug Host) is something of an Aburame clan tradition. Soon after they are born, the clan members are invaded by bugs known as Kikaichu. These bugs are raised on chakra, and their ninja hosts are able to use chakra to freely manipulate them. The Aburame are able to communicate their will to bugs, and therefore can control all such creatures. Kikaichu can form the shape of a person and confound an enemy in a way similar to Bunshin (Clone) jutsu. If one insect brushes its secretions on an enemy, other insects can detect the special insect pheromones and locate that person. Kikaichu can assist the user of the jutsu by protecting him like armor or attacking enemies with poison.

All members of the Aburame clan are experts in the study of bugs and use their knowledge of entomology to create one Kikaichu jutsu after another.

See Keyword
Kikaichu
Aburame

Why is Kiba Inazuka able to change into a beast?

The Inazuka clan that Kiba belongs to specializes in raising ninken (ninja dogs). Ninja are able to summon all kinds of animals and use them with the power of jutsu. Although ninja dogs are essentially pets that live alongside ninja, if chakra is channeled into them, they become a tool of the ninja, and can be described as a type of ningu (ninja tool).

The Inuzuka, like dogs, have a keen sense of smell, and are experts in the understanding of canines. They are adept at raising ninken and specialize in using them as ningu.

Their dogs are never far away from them, and in battle the two fight together. The Inuzuka eventually developed the Jujinka (Beast Human Transformation) that changes the human body into that of a beast.

Being able to change into trees or (as in Sunagakure) rocks in order to hide is basic jutsu, and all ninja are expert at assuming other shapes. However, being able to use four legs or attack with teeth and claws is something different altogether. The Inuzuka's canine abilities, right down to their patterns of movement, undoubtedly stem from their close association with ninken.

See Keyword

Kiba Inuzuka

43 *Why is only the main branch of the Hyuga important?*

The Hyuga are a famous family, equal in standing to Sasuke's Uchiha clan. This superiority comes from the family's control of Byakugan (White Eye) Kekkei Genkai.

The Byakugan is a very special kind of eye that expand one's field of vision, or uses the *jugen* (gentle fist) to throw an opponent's flow of chakra into disarray. It can see through the body of an opponent like an x-ray.

Depending on how it is used, the Byakugan can be even more powerful than the Uchiha clan's Sharingan, but both are genetically received and cannot be learned. This is why those in which this ability exists are highly valued and protected. A constant concern is that a clan gifted with such abilities will be targeted by someone who fears such power.

To avoid their own extinction, clan members concentrate on preserving the lives of core members. Hence the rule that clan members must sacrifice themselves to protect the clan's main branch. The Byakugan is a biological twist of fate; if the Hyuga die out then the White Eye dies with them.

This rule, however, has one flaw—the main clan members always come first, even if they have inferior skills. The relationship between Neji Hyuga and Hina Hyuga is indicative of this. Neji is an extraordinarily talented ninja with perfect control over the Byakugan. Hina isn't that great a ninja. However, Hina's birth into the main branch of the clan puts him above Neji.

ee Keyword

Hyuga
Byakugan
Kekkei Genkai
Sharingan
Neji Hyuga
Hina Hyuga

44 What is Choji's specialty, the Baika jutsu?

The fat ninja Choji usually has something in his mouth. Ninja value mobility, and therefore slim ninja are at an advantage. Choji's movements should be sluggish, handicapping him as a ninja. However, he uses the Baika (Doubling) jutsu, making being fat an advantage, and Choji's obesity now becomes an asset.

The Baika is a secret ninjutsu passed down through the Akimichi clan. It makes the body balloon by sending refined chakra into the body's cells. Choji can double his size to create a huge body mass. Using his girth to strike his opponents, he is able to put his obesity to excellent use.

The Baika jutsu consumes calories like wildfire, so Choji and the rest of the Akimichi clan are always eating to replenish them. They are experts on eating, every day studying which foods are best for replenishing calories. The results of their research can be seen in the special tablets they call *sanshoku no gan'yaku* (three colored pills). These pills are small but contain a

monstrous amount of calories. Their effectiveness
increases in order of colors: blue, yellow, and red.
The downside is that they are powerful drugs and
frequent use carries terrible risks.

See Keyword

Choji
Baika jutsu

45 *What kind of person is Sai?*

After graduating from the academy, Naruto was assigned to Team Seven, along with Sakura and Sasuke. Ninja ordinarily carry out their duties in a three-man team (although Tsunade changed the basic teams so that a medic ninja was added, forming a four-man group). Membership in the teams is fluid; members are selected based on their suitability to particular missions and duties. It is only because Naruto, Sasuke and Sakura are so well matched that their team has remained unchanged for so long.

When Sasuke left the village, the team found itself one member short. A boy named Sai was assigned to the team to replace Sasuke. Before this, Sai worked for Anbu. The members of Anbu do top secret work and usually use pseudonyms; hence "Sai" is not his real name.

Sai likes to draw and paint. He uses the Choju Giga (Super Beasts Imitation Picture) to bring his ink drawings to life. However, he has the strange inability to understand emotions, such as joy or sadness. This seems to have some connection with his upbringing, as he has had a robot-like lack of emotion since he was born. Although he studies the feelings of his fellow humans in books, he seems completely devoid of empathy.

Sai is in fact an underling of Danzo. He was assigned to Team Seven to find out what Naruto and the others are up to.

Danzo is a well-known old-timer who once opposed the Third Hokage. In contrast to the Hokage, who preached pacifism, Danzo was a warmonger. Before the Third Hokage took over, Danzo organized a special division within Anbu called Root to train Anbu members (he was probably trying to train ninja as assassins). When Sarutobi became the Third Hokage, he dissolved Root, and Danzo vacated his position as its director. But Danzo is forever dreaming of creating his ideal ninja society. To this end, a coup d'état will be necessary, and he wants to use Naruto and the Demon Fox. Therefore, he sends his own underling Sai to keep an eye on Team Seven.

At first Sai follows Danzo's orders, but his exposure to the kindness of Naruto and the others has an effect on him, and now he no longer views Danzo's orders as absolute.

See Keyword

Hebi group
Sakura
Sasuke
Sai
Choju Giga
Anbu
Danzo
Third Hokage

See Question
46

46 Who are the Anbu?

World peace has been preserved since the end of the Great Ninja World War. Opportunities for ninja to go to battle have lessened, and police work, such as pursuing murderers, is a key part of ninja activities. This law and order work has increased ninja contact with ordinary people, and today the ninja no longer have to maintain secrecy.

However, the Anbu members still uphold the ninja way of secrecy. Because they act as spies, even within their own clans, and carry out investigations at the behest of the Hokage, they are forced to operate covertly. Even while among other ninja, they conceal their faces and use pseudonyms.

See Keyword
Anbu

47 What about Asuma Sarutobi and Kurenai?

Since the time Naruto first competed in the Chunin trials, Asuma Sarutobi and Kurenai were very close, a great source of mirth for Kakashi and the others. The two were truly in love, and before anyone knew it, they were married.

Asuma Sarutobi was the son of the Third Hokage. The Third Hokage had a grandchild name Konohamaru, but Asuma was unmarried and without children. Konohamaru is the son of one of Asuma's siblings.

When the priest of the Temple of Fire (who had once worked with Asuma as one of the twelve guardian ninja) was killed by Hidan and Kakuzu, Azuma went after the killers, but they in turned killed him with their mysterious ninjutsu. However, Kurenai was already pregnant with Asuma's child. Because he has the blood of the Third Hokage, the child will probably grow up to be an outstanding ninja.

See Keyword

Asuma Sarutobi
Kurenai
Kakashi
Third Hokage
Konohamaru
Hidan
Kakuzu

See Question
16

48 Why is Shikamaru such a great strategist?

How to attain an untroubled life, according to Shikamaru, is to "become a ninja, marry a nice girl, have two kids, and after growing old, spend your time playing shogi..." To achieve this dream, he is the first among his peers to pass the Chunin trials even though he has no ambition to become a great and powerful ninja.

Shikamaru specialty is the support jutsu Kagemane (Shadow Imitation). If a battle isn't going his way, he quickly throws in the towel. However, when strategizing, he thoroughly analyzes the situation, studying the fighting ability of all combatants, then dreams up myriad tactics that repeatedly confound his opponents. In the end, he usually claims victory.

He was recognized for this refined strategic ability and progressed faster than his peers. However, he seems to have acquired this knack for strategy from his fondness for board games like *shogi*.

Shikamaru is truly gifted at playing games,

and studies his own pieces, his opponent's pieces, and his opponent's personality. He applies this way of thinking to his ninja duties, and is usually the first to come up with a strategy.

Naruto is the kind of hot-blooded guy who'll try to triumph over a stronger opponent through sheer force of will. Shikamaru isn't so full of himself, and is able to coolly and objectively analyze his own ability in battle. He formulates strategy by thinking of himself and his teammates as the playing pieces of a game, with their strengths and weaknesses in mind.

S **ee Keyword**

Shikamaru
Kagemane

49 What is Ino's specialty, the Shintenshin jutsu?

The Yamanaka are a clan who specialize in Shinjutsu (Heart Techniques), which they use to send chakra into the hearts of their opponents and take over their bodies. The Shintenshin (Mind Body Switch) jutsu used by Ino first sends chakra to the very depths of an opponent's psyche. Next, Ino cuts his own mind loose from his body and sends it plunging into the bottom of his opponent's minds. He then manipulates their bodies. For example, if his opponent has taken a hostage, Ino can use his jutsu to manipulate the opponent to set the hostage free. However, this jutsu has a downside—when used, the mind is separated from the body, leaving the body totally immobile and highly vulnerable. If the body is attacked, it can do nothing to defend itself.

Ino's father, Inoichi Yamanaka, has a higher level version of this jutsu known as Shinranshin (Mind Body Disturbance) jutsu. By sending chakra through his opponent's neural network, he can manipulate the opponent's body from afar, like remote control. The mind is not cut off from the user's body and it can still operate. Also, because it can be used on multiple targets simultaneously, it can manipulate many enemies at once and force them to attack each other.

See Keyword

Ino Yamanaka
Shintenshin
Inoichi Yamanaka
Shinranshin

Chapter 04

Mysteries of the Village of Sunagakure

50 What is the Shukaku inside Gaara?

One ninja that became a jinchuriki is Gaara. The one-tailed beast Shukaku was placed inside by his biological father (the previous Kazekage) while he was still in his mother's womb. This was done in order to turn him into a Sunagakure secret weapon.

The Shukaku is a tailed beast that has taken the form of a *tanuki* (raccoon dog). It was sealed inside a teakettle in the village of Sunagakure. It was also called *roso* ("elderly priest"), so before it was sealed away it probably assumed the form of a priest. It is said to be a skilled shape-shifter, and can take on any human image.

The Demon Fox inside Naruto is also good at assuming the human form, especially that of women. Naruto's specialty, the Oiroke ("Ninja Centerfold") jutsu, which he uses to change into the form of a sexy woman, is thought to be a utilization of the Demon Fox's power.

See Keyword

Shukaku
Gaara
Kazekage
Sunagakure

See Question

18

51 Is the previous Kazekage responsible for Gaara?

When Gaara was very young, he was greatly disturbed when told that his natural father (the previous Kazekage) had deliberately made him a monster. He also discovered that his father had tried to kill him and had never really loved him. He was tortured by loneliness and a lack of self-worth. He came to believe those who try to kill him validate his existence, that, paradoxically, those who seek to end his life gave him a reason to live.

But Gaara is wrong about his father. His father did love him. The one who actually made the decision to turn Gaara into a jinchuriki was Chiyobaa, the advisor to the previous Kazekage. In fact, Gaara is Sunagakure's third jinchuriki.

Sunagakure is part of the Land of Wind, not one of the most prosperous of places, and Sunagakure itself isn't economically blessed and therefore does not have sufficient resources to raise strong ninja. When the Great Ninja World War broke out, Sunagakure turned to the manufacture of jinchuriki as a source of ready firepower. Chiyobaa harbored special animosity toward Konohagakure because of the death of her son at the hands of Sakumo Hatake, the father of Kakashi Hatake. Her intention was probably to make a jinchuriki using Gaara to use against Konohagakure. Gaara's father chose not to oppose Chiyobaa, and Gaara was created. However, he worried that the Shukaku inside Gaara would turn him into something evil. Eventually he decided that if Gaara were to become a monster, he would have to kill him, and he began to plot a course of action. He loved Gaara more than Gaara could ever know.

See Keyword

Gaara
Kazekage
Sunagakure
Chiyobaa
Sakumo Hatake
Kakashi Hatake

See Question
04

52 What is Gaara's special Zettai Bogyo technique?

The gourd that Gaara usually carries on his back contains chakra-infused sand that has a will of its own. When Gaara is in danger, the sand leaves the gourd and surrounds his body, protecting him from attacks. This is known as Zettai Bogyo (Absolute Defense). Ordinarily, one assumes a defensive posture when an attack is imminent. But if the attack is unexpected or comes from a blind spot, injury is unavoidable. In Gaara's case, however, the sand protects him of its own free will.

Even when repeatedly attacked, Gaara is protected by the sand. The defense is impossible to penetrate, which is why it is described as an "absolute" defense.

The most outstanding aspect of Zettai Bogyo is that the sand acts totally independent of Gaara. He does not need to control it for it to do its job. It is said that the sand contains the blood of Gaara's mother, and the sand is imitating a mother's instinct to protect her child.

See Keyword

Gaara

53 What happens to Gaara if the Shukaku is removed?

After Gaara was spirited away by Akatsuki gang members Tobi and Sasori as part of their plan to seize a jinchuriki, the Shukaku inside him was removed.

When removing a tailed beast from a jinchuriki's body, it is necessary to use a sealing jutsu that consumes an amount of chakra equal to that carried by the tailed beast. The sealing jutsu used to extract the Shukaku from Gaara was called Genryu Kyufu Jin (Illusionary Dragon Nine Consuming Seal).

Jinchuriki apparently die when they lose their tailed beast's spirit, and Gaara appeared to die. However, he was revived using Chiyobaa's miraculous healing jutsu. So the death of a jinchuriki upon the loss of his tailed beast's spirit is not a sure thing.

The jutsu used by Chiyobaa to bring back Gaara was an extreme Tensei (Reincarnation) jutsu, which usually requires the sacrifice of one's own life to bring back the dead. Chiyobaa had used this resurrection kinjutsu to breathe life into her puppets.

See Keyword

Gaara
Shukaku
Akatsuki
Chakra
Jinchuriki
Chiyobaa

54 Why does Sunagakure view Konohagakure as its rival?

The Land of Fire where the village of Konohagakure is located borders the Land of Wind in which Sunagakure is located. The two have been rivals for what seems like forever. They fought many battles during the Great Ninja World War, which saw Chiyobaa's son killed by Sakumo Hatake, the White Fang of Konohagakure.

After the war, the Land of Fire and Land of Wind formed an alliance that inadvertently led the village of Sunagakure to lose some of its power. This was because the daimyo of the Land of Wind decided on a military reduction policy.

In contrast, the daimyo of the Land of Fire established a policy through which he could profit. By favoring Konohagakure, he enabled it to produce strong ninja that could be hired out to other countries in times of war. Now, with the village of Sunagakure in its weakened state, requests for support of the ninja of Konohagakure have become frequent.

Some, like Chiyobaa, deplore the current

state of affairs in which Sunagakure must rely on Konohagakure, with which it had so violently fought in the past. They view Konohagakure as a rival. They want Sunagakure to become strong again so that it never has to rely on another country.

However, Gaara is the new Kazekage of Sunagakure and, being on good terms with Naruto, he has made sure Sunagakure and Konohagakure have a relationship based on friendship. This drives Chiyobaa and her ilk up the wall, and deepens their hatred of Konohagakure all the more.

See Keyword

Sunagakure
Konohagakure
Chiyobaa
Sakumo Hatake
Gaara

55 Did Chiyobaa develop the Kugutsu jutsu?

The specialty of Kankuro is the Kugutsu (Puppet) jutsu, although it is a Sunagakure tradition. Kankuro is famous for this jutsu, but he seems to have somehow learned it from Chiyobaa. Chiyobaa doesn't just manipulate puppets with chakra extending from her fingertips. She is also a skilled at attaching chakra to the hands and feet of humans, effectively turning them into puppets.

There are two kinds of ninjutsu—one is developed by an individual ninja and popularized; another is genetically inherited. It is not clear if Chiyobaa invented the Kugutsu jutsu herself, or learned it. However, it doesn't seem to be a genetically-enabled jutsu, as there are other ninja in Sunagakure who can use it, such as Sasori (Chiyobaa's grandchild), who was in Akatsuki, and Kankuro (who has no blood ties with Chiyobaa).

This jutsu doesn't just require the chakra that extends in threads from the fingertips, but also puppets. It is improbable that Chiyobaa could have perfected the development of puppets herself; Kugutsu seems to have been refined over many generations. The puppets were probably developed by past ninja, and Chiyobaa herself was taught the jutsu and the making of puppets by her elders.

See Keyword

Chiyobaa
Kugutsu
Kankuro
Sunagakure
Sasori
Akatsuki

56 Who made the puppets that Kankuro uses?

The most famous user of the Kugutsu (Puppet) jutsu in Sunagakure is Kankuro, but he didn't make his most important puppet, Karasu. The puppets he uses were made by Chiyobaa's grandchild, Sasori, a member of Akatsuki who assassinated the Third Kazekage and fled Sunagakure.

Kankuro is an expert Kugutsu jutsu user, but he doesn't seem to be all that great at developing puppets. Only Chiyobaa and her grandchild Sasori had such knowledge.

See Keyword

Kankuro
Sunagakure
Karasu
Chiyobaa
Sasori

57 Is Temari the only one to use the giant fan weapon?

B ig sister of Kankuro and Gaara, Temari specializes in a jutsu that comprises a strong wind created by a gigantic fan.

Temari has the wind-nature chakra, but so have many other ninja from the Land of Wind, where Sunagakure is located. The country is mostly desert. Over these sands strong winds constantly blow. Many of the ninjutsu developed there take advantage of the power of the wind. Outsiders who specialize in wind Seishitsu Henka are drawn to Sunagakure because of its windiness.

Although Temari is the only ninja who appears using a giant fan, Sunagakure must have other such ninja.

See Keyword

Temari
Kankuro
Gaara
Sunagakure

Chapter 05

Secrets of
Otogakure

58 Why does Orochimaru establish the village of Otogakure?

After failing to achieve his goal of becoming the Fourth Hokage, Orochimaru left the village and established his own, known as Otogakure, with the ultimate aim of destroying Konohagakure.

Ordinarily, ninja villages form a pact with their country's daimyo, or feudal ruler, and take on military duties in exchange for financial support. National defense is a ninja village's raison d'être.

Orochimaru's village is different. It was created with the goal of bringing about a coup d'état, and receives no assistance from the daimyo. It does accept commissions from small countries that have no ninja. Interestingly, it participated in the Chunin trials, a fact that would suggest it is recognized as a proper ninja village.

Otogakure has another purpose—it acts as a prison laboratory where Orochimaru carries out experiments on live humans.

Orochimaru has bases in Otogakure where he holds captives kidnapped from neighboring villages. These he uses in his cursed seal experiments.

See Keyword

Orochimaru
Otogakure
Fourth Hokage
Konohagakure

59 Why does Kabuto Yakushi follow Orochimaru?

Most of the ninja in Otogakure have been given cursed seals by Orochimaru, and are therefore unable to defy him. However, Kabuto Yakushi has been given no such seal, but he still respects Orochimaru and follows him loyally.

Kabuto was left as an orphan after the Great Ninja World War. A medic ninja from Konohagakure took pity on him, took him back to the village, and raised him as his own son. Who this ninja was, it is not known, but Kabuto was brought up in Konohagakure and studied ninjutsu there. He is recorded as a ninja resident of Konohagakure, and he has competed in the Chunin trials a number of times as a Konohagakure ninja. However, it turns out his participation in the trials was on the orders of Orochimaru as a surveillance operation. Orochimaru's plan was to zero in on certain ninja at the trials, put cursed seals on them, and make them his own.

It is apparent that Kabuto has been a faithful

subject of Orochimaru for a long time, although the details are sketchy as to why Kabuto betrayed Konohagakure, which raised him, and turned to Orochimaru, whose goal is to destroy the village. One suggestion is that Kabuto, as a healing ninja, is fascinated by Orochimaru's Furo Fushi (Immortality) research, seeing it as revolutionary.

When Orochimaru dies at the hands of Sasuke, Kabuto transplants some of Orochimaru's cells into his own body. The cells boost Kabuto's strength, but are now trying to take over his body. Close to 30 percent of Kabuto's body has already been taken over by Orochimaru.

See Keyword

Kabuto Yakushi
Orochimaru
Otogakure
Konohagakure
Sasuke

60 Why didn't Kimimaro become Orochimaru's next body?

The sole survivor of the Kaguya clan, Kimimaro possesses a Kekkei Genkai that allows him to create new bones. Orochimaru saw him as his next incarnation. Kimimaro is a good-looking guy and he has a Kekkei Genkai, so he was probably considered a real catch for the narcissistic Orochimaru. However, when Kimimaro falls ill, Orochimaru realizes that he must find a substitute to where his soul can transmigrate. So Orochimaru turns his thoughts to Sasuke. But again his plans are stymied, and he has to make do with someone else.

One would expect members of the Kaguya clan, with their remarkable power, to be the superior of the ninja groups, and so we must question how it was that they were all killed in battle. One theory is that the Kekkei Genkai that allows them to form new bones carries with it a disease gene that has been passed through the generations, and has led to the near total annihilation of the group.

See Keyword

Kimimaro
Orochimaru
Kekkei Genkai
Sasuke

61 Why does Kidomaru look like a spider?

Among the Sound Four, the one whose cursed seal has had the most noticeable effects is Kidomaru. The power of the seal turns him into a six-armed, demonic man-spider.

Orochimaru, through repeated experiments, perfected cursed seal jutsu that cause bodily transformations, synthesizing human and animal forms. Kidomaru can change his body into a spider-like form because he has been given this kind of cursed seal. Kidomaru can spew up chakra like a spider, and can make spider webs to capture his enemies. And by making the sticky chakra threads hard as steel, he can create ad hoc metallic weapons.

Jinchuriki combine the powers of tailed beasts with the abilities of the human vessel. They are able to acquire unique powers unattainable to normal humans. Orochimaru's research is thought to have been an attempt to attain the same effect by way of cursed seal jutsu. By creating a ninja like Kidomaru, who not only has the shape of a spider but can also use a spider's unique abilities, he succeeded.

See Keyword

Kidomaru
Jinchuriki
Orochimaru

62 What special talents do Sakon and Ukon have?

The spirits of the twins, Sakon and Ukon, ordinarily inhabit a single body. Thus, they can channel the chakra of two people, and, while one is at rest, the other can attack (this is called a fukyuu fumin or "no rest no sleep" battle), making them formidable ninja. Also, the older brother Ukon can leave the body and possess a third party's body, right down to the cellular level. This is because Ukon has the ability to fuse his cells with those of another person.

These powers are believed to be possible because the twins were given a cursed seal developed by Orochimaru that does not fuse the body of a human with an animal, but with another human. Sakon has the ability to fuse with people and freely destroy or revive their bodies cell by cell.

Sakon and Ukon are normally one body with two separate minds, and when the two minds are in conflict, they are able to see themselves objectively. Thus, they are suited to leadership in a similar way to that of Shikamaru.

See Keyword

Sakon
Ukon
Orochimaru
Shikamaru

63 What special abilities does Jirobo have?

It's easy to imagine Jirobo, who looks like a sumo wrestler, as having superhuman strength. When his cursed seal reaches level 2, all that changes are his facial features and the color of his skin; he does not take on the traits of an animal, as the others do. All the cursed seal probably does is amplify his power.

His distinguishing trait is his ability to make a dome-like structure from earth, trap people inside it, and suck away their chakra, making it his own. This jutsu has the defect of consuming much of his body's normal energy (i.e., calories) while channeling chakra, sometimes causing his body's calorie levels to fall dangerously low. In this way, he is similar to Choji. However, unlike Choji, Jirobo chooses not to maintain chakra by replenishing calories through eating, but by absorbing the chakra of his opponents.

Jirobo is eventually killed in a fight with Choji, who was able to pull this off thanks to the power of the Akimichi clan's secret tradition, the sanshoku no gan'yaku (three-color pills).

See Keyword

Jirobo
Chakra
Choji

64 What special powers does Tayuya have?

nother ninja of the Sound Four who has been given a cursed seal is Tayuya. When Tayuya's cursed seal reaches level 2, she sprouts horns from her head and her physical power dramatically increases. However, she has one shortcoming—most of her talents are long-distance genjutsu attacks, and her increase in strength never really comes into play. She hasn't been that lucky with the seal she was given.

She uses a flute to cast her ninjutsu spells, which she can do at almost any distance from the target. When casting genjutsu with the Sharingan (Copy Wheel Eye), for example, it is necessary to show one's eyes to one's opponent. However, when using sound-derived genjutsu like Tayuya's, it is possible to cast the jutsu without even turning up for the fight. She also has the power to summon subordinates with her flute that she manipulates with her instrument.

Because of her determined, unyielding spirit, she felt compelled to show herself before Shikamaru. However, Shikamaru analyzed the motions of her fingers as she played and predicted the pattern of her attack. Tayuya's ultimate blunder was trying to prove herself to Shikamaru.

See Keyword

Tayuya
Shikamaru

Chapter 06

Secrets of Akatsuki

65 What is Akatsuki's interest in jinchuriki?

The mysterious group Akatsuki has set its sights on the jinchuriki, which are scattered throughout the world. Because there are nine tailed beasts, with the number of tails from one to nine, it is thought that, including Naruto, there are nine jinchuriki. The members of Akatsuki intend to develop a devastatingly powerful weapon by removing the spirits of the tailed beasts from the jinchuriki and using their immense power. They extracted the one-tailed Shukaku's spirit from Gaara and the spirit of the Two Tailed Demon Cat from a jinchuriki named Yugito, a ninja from Kirigakure. Other tailed beasts have been captured by Akatsuki, and the group has also targeted Naruto and his Nine Tailed Demon Fox.

By developing such a weapon, they hope to grow rich through warfare. This effectively makes them the first group of soldiers of fortune in the world of ninja. They plan to use this new organization as a hired gun to reap enormous rewards.

Akatsuki's first goal is to gain total control over all warfare; its ultimate goal is world domination. With its all-powerful weaponry, it plans to conquer the world, eliminate war, and achieve world peace.

See Keyword

Akatsuki
Jinchuriki
Shukaku
Gaara
Nine Tailed Demon Fox

See Question
66

66 How does Akatsuki recruit new members?

I n the same way that Itachi scouted Deidara, new members of Akatsuki come on board by being recruited by those who are already members. The particulars of how Itachi and Kisame joined Akatsuki are not known. It may be that Itachi knew something of Akatsuki, sympathized with its cause, and subsequently slaughtered his entire clan.

Orochimaru has belonged to Akatsuki for a very long time ago, meaning Akatsuki itself is an organization of long standing. Its members hail from a variety of locales—Itachi is from Konohagakure, Sasori from Sunagakure, and Kisame from Kirigakure. The group probably conducts clandestine surveillance of the many villages in search of disgruntled ninja to recruit.

Akatsuki only really became widely known when it started actively searching for jinchuriki. Its members did scout new recruits until the organization grew to a certain size, but now it is largely set up and in place, their true purpose has been revealed.

S ee Keyword

Deidara
Kisame
Itachi
Orochimaru
Konohagakure
Sasori
Sunagakure
Kirigakure
Jinchuriki

See Question

66

67 How many members does Akatsuki have?

The core members of Atsuki are Itachi, Kisame Hoshigaki, Sasori, the worker of puppets, Deidara, the Bakudanma ("bombing devil"), the mysterious ninja Zetsu, whose face is covered with what looks like the leaf of a carnivorous plant, Kakuzu, a man who has faith in nothing but money, Tobi, who wears a "whirlpool" mask, and Hidan, the follower of a cult that teaches salvation through mass murder.

The organization is believed to have at the very least ten members, many of whom are from the village of Amegakure. Beginning with Sasori, there has been a number who have died. Their meetings, to which only their minds attend, are always held in a cave-like environment. Because they do not physically meet at these gatherings, not all those in Akatsuki are familiar with their fellow members.

They seem to usually work in groups of two when carrying out operations: Kisame and Itachi, Kakuzu and Hidan. These operations are not restricted to just hunting jinchuriki; they also pay close to attention to the activities of Sasuke and Orochimaru.

See Keyword

Atsuki
Itachi
Kisame Hoshigaki
Sasori
Deidara
Zetsu
Kakuzu
Hidan
Amegakure

See Question
68

68 *Who is the leader of Akatsuki?*

The alleged leader of Akatsuki provides instructions to the group's members from above a stone statue in the middle of the cave. At the time of the creation of Akatsuki, a parliamentary system in which plans were decided on through dialogue was in place (even the anti-authoritarian Orochimaru allowed himself to become a member). However, now that Akatsuki is active, a single leader plans strategy and the members act in accordance with his or her orders. This leader of Akatsuki has yet to reveal his or her identity, but rumor has it that it may be a ninja from Amegakure.

It is also rumored that Tobi, who joined after Sasori's death to make up the numbers, may be pulling the strings. Tobi's true identity is that of ninja Madara Uchiha, who is considered the founder of the Uchiha clan. It was once thought that there were no surviving members of the Uchiha clan other than Sasuke and Itachi, but it is now known that because Madara still lives there are at least three of them. It isn't known how a man from an ancient era said to have been the genesis of the Uchiha clan can still be alive. However, it is said that Madara is able to use jutsu to summon the Nine Tailed Demon Fox, and so the Demon Fox sealed within Naruto probably knows all about him.

See Keyword

Akatsuki
Orochimaru
Amegakure
Sasori
Tobi
Madara Uchiha
Sasuke
Itachi
Nine Tailed Demon Fox

See Question
67

140

69 What kind of place is the village of Amegakure?

The village of Amegakure occupies a position between the Land of Fire, the Land of Earth, and the Land of Wind. Because of this geographical characteristic, it finds itself at the center of conflicts between the great nations, and often serves as a battlefield. However, because of the efforts of its leader, the legendary ninja Sanshouo Hanzo (Salamander Hanzo), it wasn't destroyed at the time of the Great War and today continues to function as a small but successful village-state. However, because of its unique position, it is always on guard. It carries out exhaustive inspections of people entering and leaving, and monitors those who remain. Also, through a thorough control of information, secrets from within Amegakure are never leaked.

According to information collected by Jiraiya, Hanzo was the former chief, but the current leader is a man named Pein. A civil war rages between sides loyal to each of the leaders, cutting the village in half. But because of the village's secretiveness, almost no outsiders are aware of this.

Further investigations by Jiraiya reveal that Hanzo's former authority as chief has been nullified, and his household all massacred. What's more, the new chieftain Pein is being revered by the people as a deity. With Pein a member of Akatsuki, there is the likelihood that the real base of the organization is somewhere is Amegakure.

See Keyword

Amegakure

Hanzo

Jiraiya

Pein

Akatsuki

70 *What is Deidara's specialty?*

As a user of Earth Release jutsu, Deidara can create clay with chakra that can be shaped into living creatures. Deidara is a self-styled artiste and will only work his clay into shapes of his liking. He seems especially taken with birds, and makes a lot of them. There is a mouth-like opening on each of his palms from where he squeezes out the chakra clay. However, this jutsu does not reflect his true nature.

Deidara sees explosion as art, and from the clay he makes bombs. The bombs he makes are classified into levels ranging from C1 to C4. There is a great deal of variation in these weapons. Some are dropped from the sky, some are landmines; others are time-bombs, and so on. The self-styled "bomb artist" Deidara sees bombs as his reason for living.

His most dangerous bomb is the nanosized C4 Karura ("Griffin"). It is the size of an atom, and care must be taken to avoid inhaling it. If it is inhaled, it enters the cells where it detonates. The unfortunate victim is blown to smithereens, with only a trace of smoke remaining.

See Keyword

Deidara
Chakra
Sharingan

When Deidara views illusions at the hands of Itachi's Sharingan (Copy Wheel Eye), he believes them to be more beautiful than his own works of art. This leads him to develop a complex about the Sharingan, and he eventually trains his left eye not to see the Sharingan illusions. This makes him one of the select few against whom the Sharingan is useless.

71 How did Hidan survive decapitation?

The special skill of Hidan, known as Gishiki (Ceremony), requires a curious procedure.

First, blood is taken from an opponent trying to use jutsu; second, a ring is drawn on the ground using chakra; third, jutsu is brought into action from within the circle.

In Hidan's case, his physical pain is synchronized with that of his opponent. Within the circle, Hidan inflicts injuries on himself, and in the exact same manner, his opponent's body suffers injuries. If Hidan stabs his heart while he is within the circle, his opponent's heart is pierced in the same manner, with the result being death. However, Hidan is immortal, and therefore never dies.

Even after decapitation, Hidan will continue to live, with the severed head eventually reattaching to the body. How this is possible is not explained, but he was probably born with a Kekkei Genkai that gives him a miraculous life force.

See Keyword

Hidan
Chakra
Kekkei Genkai

72 Why does Kakuzu have five hearts?

With his remarkable body, Kakuzu attacks opponents by extending tentacles from within him. By detaching his arms and legs, he can attach them to the tentacles and attack opponents from afar. However, the most extraordinary aspect of Kakuzu's body is that he has five hearts. Because of this, he has a singularly strong life force. If an opponent wants to kill Kakuzu, the opponent must destroy all five of his hearts. In other words, he has the life force of five men.

Kakuzu can remove hearts from living people and place them into his own body. This makes him essentially immortal. He claims to have fought against the First Hokage and is certainly very old. However, because he can replace his hearts with fresh ones, the ageing process is of no concern to him.

On top of this, when he takes an opponent's heart, he can tap into its chakra channel and steal his victim's special chakra nature. Hypothetically speaking, if Kakuzu takes the hearts of ninja who have earth, wind, fire, water, and lightning chakra natures, then he could become the ultimate chakra master.

See Keyword

Kakuzu
First Hokage
Chakra

73 Who is Madara Uchiha?

Thought to be the original member of the Uchiha clan, Madara Uchiha is believed to have been the first to develop the Sharingan (Copy Wheel Eye). Rumor has it that he is still living, and that Akatsuki member Tobi and Madara are one and the same.

It is also rumored that Madara can use summoning jutsu, and may have been the one who called up the Nine Tailed Demon Fox now sealed within Naruto. Tailed beasts are thought to appear in a vortex in the ground when the wickedness of man reaches a certain level. This is usually followed by total destruction of the area. If Madara can summon tailed beasts, then the destruction of Konohagakure by the Demon Fox may have, in fact, been a manmade disaster.

Madara is also another possible candidate for Akatsuki's true puppet master. If this is true, then Akatsuki's goal may not be world conquest, but something entirely different.

See Keyword

Madara Uchiha
Sharingan
Akatsuki
Tobi
Nine Tailed Demon Fox
Konohagakure

74 Who is the legendary ninja, Sennin Rikido?

The man believed responsible for the basics of all present-day ninjutsu was known as Sennin Rikido. He is said to be the forerunner of all ninja. Sennin Rikido had Rinnegan (Transmigration Eye), a special eye that eventually developed into the Sharingan (Copy Wheel Eye) of the Uchiha clan, and the Byakugan (White Eye) of the Hyuga clan.

Sennin Rikido's actual existence has never been established, and stories of him are thought to be just legends. However, Pein, who is the new leader of the village of Amegakure, has the same eye. It is because of this that Jiraiya and others believe Rikido Sennin really did exist, and Pein is his descendant.

When Jiraiya was young, Amegakure was at war. At the time, Jiraiya knew Pein as an orphan named Nagato. Jiraiya looked after and taught Nagato and two other orphans (Konan and Yahiko) for three years. Jiraiya was shocked when he found out that Nagato, the orphan he had raised, had become Pein, the central figure of

Akatsuki.

See Keyword

Sennin Rikido
Rinnegan
Sharingan
Byakugan
Amegakure
Pein
Jiraiya
Nagato
Akatsuki

GLOSSARY

Characters

Konohagakure: The Village Hidden in the Leaves (The Land of Fire)

Naruto Uzumaki

The main character of the saga. The Nine Tailed Demon Fox is sealed within his body. His parents are gone, and he is persecuted by the adults of the village as the reincarnation of the Demon Fox. He spends his childhood in isolation and dreams of becoming a Hokage. He has an extraordinarily strong sense of esprit de corps, and because of this is able to attract many sympathizers. Because he is able to use the chakra of the Demon Fox to his advantage, he specializes in techniques such as the Rasengan (Spiraling Sphere) and Kage Bunshin (Shadow Clone) that utilize enormous amounts of chakra. This chakra has the essence of wind, and he personally develops the Rasen Shuriken (Spiral Shuriken) ninjutsu, which alters the nature of the wind in the Rasengan. Since he has the Demon Fox sealed within his body, no matter how much injury he sustains, he quickly recovers. However, he carries the risk of losing control over himself if he gives in to violent emotions such as anger and the spirit of the Demon Fox is released from him.

Sasuke Uchiha

Naruto's rival. He earns the highest grades of Naruto's academy classmates. After graduating, he begins his duties as a member of Naruto's team. Has the Sharingan (Copy Wheel Eye), which appears exclusively among the Uchiha clan. His specialty is Genjutsu. Because the chakra of the Uchiha clan has the essence of fire, he is also adept at using the Katon (Fire Release) jutsu. Also, having learned the Chidori (One Thousand Birds) jutsu from Kakashi, he has mastered the transformation of fire's essence. Since his entire clan, including his parents, are killed by his older brother Itachi, he sees vengeance as his life's most important objective. He has no qualms about betraying his friends to achieve this goal. Orochimaru decides to take over Sasuke's body and gives him the Juin (Cursed Seal) jutsu. Sasuke can alter his body in ways such as sprouting wings. He seeks revenge from Orochimaru, and kills him. He is accompanied by the three ninja (Jugo, Karin and Suigetsu) that were in Orochimaru's hideout and, under the name Hebi (lit. snake), the team goes after its prey—Itachi.

Sakura Haruno

A classmate of Naruto and a member of Team Seven. Haruno is adroit at cultivating chakra, and the wielder of an intelligence through which she quickly masters new ninjutsu. This ability is discovered by the Fifth Hokage Tsunade, and Sakura is presently developing into an excellent iryou (healing) ninja. Using the supernatural power she receives from Tsunade, she knocks Naruto out cold whenever Naruto does something like tell a stupid joke.

Kakashi Hatake

The captain of Team Seven consisting of Naruto and the others. He usually goes by the name of Sharingan no Kakashi. He is called a "copy ninja"; using the Sharingan in his left eye, he can view the techniques used by his enemies and make those techniques his own. The Sharingan, which normally only appears in members of the Uchiha clan, is carried in Kakashi's left eye because it was transplanted from his good friend Obito Uchiha. He is the son of Sakumo Hatake, who, under the nom de guerre Shiroi Kiba ("White Fang"), put the fear in ninja throughout the world

Sai

Real name unclear. He was assigned to Team Seven to make up for the loss of Sasuke. A subordinate of Danzo in the Anbu training division Root, Danzo tells him to keep an eye on Team Seven's mainstay Naruto, and orders him to assassinate Sasuke. However, he is touched by the humanity of Naruto and the others and now acts in accordance with his own thoughts. His specialty is the

Choju Giga (lit. super beasts imitation picture) ninjutsu, which brings the pictures he draws to life.

Danzo

Once stood in opposition to the Third Hokage. In contrast with the Third Hokage, who preached pacifism, he advocates warmongering. He organizes the separate Anbu training department Root within Anbu. Root is now disbanded and Danzo has retired from his position within it, but he is secretly plotting a coup d'état through which he will make Konohagakure into his ideal village. For this reason, he recommends Sai for membership in Team Seven, and among other things orders Sai to assassinate Sasuke, cooperate with Orochimaru, and keep an eye on Naruto.

Tenzo (Yamato)

A ninja who carries the genes of the First Hokage. The sole survivor of Orchimaru's experiments performed on 60 infants who carried the genetic material of the First Hokage. Can use the Tree Release jutsu that only the First Hokage could use. He is well versed in techniques for sealing tailed beasts and pacifies the Demon Fox whenever it runs wild.

Sarutobi

The instructor in charge of Team Ten. Jonin. Like Naruto, his chakra has the nature of wind. A talented man who is selected for the former 12 shugonin (

"guardian ninja"), a group of special guardsmen who protect the Daimyo. The son of the Third Hokage, he marries Kurenai. He is expected to soon become a father after Kurenai becomes pregnant, but is killed by his own jutsu.

Shikamaru Nara

With his habit of saying "what a drag," he rarely hides his apathy, but is in fact a tactician with an IQ of 200. He implements strategy on the battlefield in a cool and collected manner. He specializes in jutsu that use shadows to bind opponents, like the Kageshibari (Shadow Freeze) and the Kagemane (Shadow Copy).

Ino Yamanaka

The only girl in Asuma's team, she is both the best friend and greatest rival of Sakura. Her specialty is the Shintenshin jutsu, used to enter the minds of others.

Choji Akimichi

He is distinguished by his bloated physique, which results from his constant eating. If called "fat," he fills with uncontrollable rage. His specialty is the Baika (Doubling) jutsu, which allows his body to balloon.

Might Guy

The instructor in charge of Team Guy. He has a fiery spirit, but is thought of by those other than Rock to be a little too intense. He trains himself so he can defeat his rival Kakashi.

Rock Lee

The adoring pupil of Might Guy. Since ninjutsu are not his forte, he is a unique sort of ninja who specializes in taijutsu only. He believes without doubt that if you try, you can do anything. Even after reaching exhaustion point, he can continue to fight through sheer force of will. Using the Hachimon (Eight Gates) forbidden jutsu to release the eight-point limit within his body, he repeatedly performs taijutsu that are beyond his physical limitations. Because of this, his body is battered and crushed, and he is forced to give up being a ninja, but miraculously recovers thanks to medic ninja Tsunade.

Hyuga Neji

Born into a branch of the Hyuga clan, he wields the Kekkei Genkai Byakugan (White Eye), which only members of that clan possess. Neji can use it to see through his opponents, attacking their chakra points and destroying their internal organs with the juken (gentle fist) technique.

Tenten

The sole female member of Team Guy, she has a chignon hairdo as her distinguishing trait. Usually wears traditional Chinese clothing. She is the only specialist of ningu attacks among Team Guy, who mostly use taijutsu. In close combat she can use staff techniques and the like. Specializes in summoning scrolls to make useable ningu materialize.

Kurenai Yuhi

The female instructor in charge of Team Eight. She is a topflight user of genjutsu. She marries Asuma and becomes pregnant with his child, but Asuma is killed before the child is born.

Kiba Inazuka

A youth from the Inazuka clan who specializes in fighting with his dog. He has a keen sense of smell and the intuition of a wild animal. He has a fierce temperament and a wild nature. He acts on instinct rather than relying on logic. He goes on daily walks with his dog and is an expert on the geography of his village. In battle, he uses refined but remarkably effective attacks. The Gatsuga (Double Piercing Fang), which he performs in cooperation with Akamaru, is a lethal technique.

Tsume Inazuka

The mother of Kiba. Training ninja dogs is her specialty, and because of this, she holds a special Jonin ranking.

Hana Inazuka

The older sister of Kiba. She is an excellent veterinarian.

Shino Aburame

A youth from the Aburame clan who has made a name for himself through the use of bugs. By forming a pact that allows him to allot his chakra as fodder for bugs, he is able to utilize destructive bugs in manifold ways: attack, defense, healing, searching, pursuit, capture, etc. He specializes in a cerebral kind of fighting through which he adroitly puts the nature of bugs to good use, and is adept at analyzing battles in the same way as Shikamaru.

Shibi Aburame

A member of the Aburame clan who has made a name for himself through the use of bugs. The father of Shino, he is usually researching the nature of bugs, and develops new destructive vermin. In the anime he is known as "Gen".

Hinata Hyuga

Born into the main branch of the Hyuga clan. Has a weak spirit, and it cannot be said with any conviction that she is suited for the role of ninja. However, as she is born into the main branch of the clan everyone expects her to become a powerful ninja. She is a user of the Kekkei Genkai Byakugan (White Eye), which enables her to see her opponent's chakra. Because she has a passive nature and gives up easily, she is seen as inferior to her little sister Hanabi. Her father Hizashi has given up on her. Though Neji's ability is vastly superior, Neji is viewed as Hinata's inferior because Hinata is a member of the main branch of the clan. Neji resents Hinata, but they reconcile their differences. Because she is a fundamentally weak and shy person, in fights with Neji, she suffers. Nevertheless, she is not a quitter. She is fond of Naruto.

Hizashi Hyuga

The head of the main Hyuga clan. He is the twin of Hizashi from a branch of the clan. As the eldest brother, he became part of the main branch, while his brother didn't, which has left him wracked with guilt.

Hanabi Hyuga

A member of the main Hyuga clan. She is the little sister of Hinata. She has greater ability as a ninja than Hinata; this is one of the reasons why she has developed a complex about Hinata.

Hizashi Hyuga

From a branch of the Hyuga clan. He is the twin of Hizashi, the head of the main branch. In accordance with the rules of the Hyuga clan that view only the main branch as important, his life is sacrificed to spare his brother.

Shodai (First) Hokage

The great founder of Konohagakure. He is the only ninja who could use Tree Release techniques such as Jukai Kotan (Birth of Dense Woodland). Sees the people of his village as if they are a part of his own body and overflows with feelings for them. He is the uncle of the Fifth Hokage Tsunade. He seems to have had a war with Kabuto of Akatsuki in the past. He is said to have defeated Madara Uchiha, the founder of the Uchiha clan, at Shumatsu no Tani ("the Valley of the End"). Brought back to life by Orochimaru's summoning jutsu So Tensei (Impure World Resurrection), he fights the Third Hokage.

Second Hokage

The younger brother of the First Hokage. He is the founder of the ninja academy. He is a specialist of Water Release techniques and can use them even in places where no water is present. In contrast to his composed brother, he has a feverish temperament and presses on unflinchingly toward his goals. Along with the First Hokage, he is resurrected by the jutsu of Orochimaru and does battle with the Third Hokage.

Sarutobi, the Third Hokage

Said to be the most powerful Hokage in all history. He was the pupil of the First and Second Hokage. His actual ability is considerable in spite of his age, and because he is able to use all the jutsu existing in Konohagakure, he has the sobriquet "Professor." He is an excellent leader, and the ninja training curriculum he proposed is still in use even today. He trained the trio (Jiraiya, Tsunade, and Orochimaru) who came to be known as the three legendary ninja. He is a great ninja who loves the village and protects those who live there. During his reign, he relinquishes the title of Hokage, but after the death of his successor, he reclaims the title. When Orochimaru invades Konohagakure, Sarutobi defends the village from his attacks and loses his life in the process. He is the father of Asuma.

Minato Kamikaze, the Fourth Hokage

Over a decade ago, after fighting the Nine Tailed Demon Fox, which had destroyed Konohagakure, Minato seals the Nine Tailed Demon Fox within Naruto using the Shiki Fujin (Dead Demon Consuming Seal) technique, and pays for this with his life. He is known as "Konohagakure's Great Yellow Flash," and during the time of the Third Great Ninja World War, he seems to have been greatly feared by the ninja of other villages.

Tsunade, the Fifth Hokage

One of the three legendary ninja. She becomes the Fifth Hokage after the death of the Third. She is a specialist of healing jutsu, but after losing her little brother Nawaki and her lover Dan in war, she begins to have doubts about the ninja way of life and leaves the village for a while. After becoming the Fifth Hokage, she changes the existing three-ninja-team system so that every team has at least one healing ninja. Since her specialization is in healing and resurrection jutsu, it may be because she uses these techniques on her body that she is able to maintain such a youthful appearance in spite of her real age being in excess of 50 years.

Shizune

A pupil and retainer of Tsunade. She is always doing things together with Tsunade, and is one of the few Tsunade trusts. After Tsunade assumes the role of Hokage, Shizune still follows her around and supports her like a secretary. She has excellent skills as a healing Jonin. She is

the niece of Tsunade's deceased lover Dan.

Choza Akimichi

The father of Choji. Together with Shikaku and Inoichi, he is part of the Ino-Shika-Cho formation. He is an even bigger glutton than his son. His weapon is the Baika (Doubling) jutsu.

Shikaku Nara

The father of Shikamaru. He is part of the Ino-Shika-Cho formation with Choza and Inoichi. He is a henpecked husband and is no match for his wife. In the scene where he roars at Shikamaru, we get a glimpse of his true ferocity. In games of shogi, his skill exceeds that of Shikamaru.

Inoichi Yamanaka

The father of Ino. Together with Shikaku and Choza, he is once part of the Ino-Shika-Cho formation. He is a rather doting parent who fawns over his only daughter, Ino.

Ebisu

A Tokubetsu (Special) Jonin who works as an elite tutor and grooms candidates for the next Hokage. At first he refers to Naruto as the "Demon Fox brat" and views him with hostility, but later gives him recognition and sometimes takes part in Naruto's training.

Ibiki Morino

The commanding officer of Konoha Torture and Interrogation Force. Because of his exacting style of torture and interrogation, he is also known by the nickname "Sadist." He appears as a judge the first time Naruto competes in the Chunin trials.

Anko Mitarashi

A former pupil of Orochimaru. She is branded with the Ten no Juin (Cursed Seal of Heaven) by Orochimaru. She serves as the judge at the second trial (The Trial of the Forest of Death), the first time Naruto competes in the Chunin trials. She tries to sacrifice her own life to kill Orochimaru but fails. She is distinguished by her bold statements and actions, but she seems to lack intuition. She is quite the sweet-tooth, and during the recess period in the Chunin trials, she gobbles up 53 dango (dumplings) and sucks down a can of shiruko (sweet bean soup). She uses the Sen'ei Jashu (Hidden Shadow Snake Hand) technique also used by Orochimaru.

Genma Shiranui

Serves as the judge at the third match of the Chunin trials the first time Naruto competes in them. He usually acts cool and aloof from the world but his actual skill level is high, and his Senbon (One Thousand Needles) has the power to offset the force of a kunai (a long, pointed Japanese weapon).

Raido Namaishi

Teams up with Genma, Shizune and Iishi during the execution of his duties. He has scars from burns he sustained to his face. He has a sense of right and wrong so strong it even compels him to interrupt correspondence between the Hokage and Kazekage. Raido forms a four-man cell with Choji, Ino and Aoba after the creation of 20 new small teams. He rushes to the aid of Team Asuma, but is a moment too late and has to watch Asuma die. He uses the Kokuto ("Black Sword").

Hayate Gekko

The judge of the third preliminary match the first time Naruto challenges the Chunin trials. He has a weak constitution and is always coughing. He loses his life in battle with the Sunagakure Jonin Baki.

Tonbo Tobitake

The proctor for the initial trail of the Chunin trials the first time Naruto challenges them. He has his head wrapped in a headband. He displays fierce emotions when his pride is on the line, and chastises the Sunagakure Genin Komaza when Komaza flunks the trials.

Aoba Yamashiro

Wears sunglasses and, no matter what, is always cool and collected. He forms a four-man cell with Raido, Choji, and Ino after the creation of the 20 new small teams. Rushes to the aid of Team Asuma, but is a moment too late and bears witness to Asuma's death. He uses

Toriyose (Bird Summoning) jutsu.

Iruka Umino

An instructor at the village academy set up to train the ninja who will serve as the village's military might. He had a rough childhood following the deaths of his parents at the hands of the Nine Tailed Demon Fox. He was the first to recognize the life-long loner Naruto as not just a strong warrior but a human being, and is one of the few who understands Naruto well. Iruka lives as if he is Naruto's protector, to the extent that at the Valley of the End he is told by Naruto, "if my father were around I would feel the same way about him as I feel about you."

Mizuki

A former instructor at the ninja academy. He is a superficially affable person but is in reality ambitious. Tricks Naruto into stealing the kinjutsu scrolls (and this incident serves as the impetus for Naruto mastering the Kage Bunshin (Shadow Clone) kinjutsu). Tries to kill Naruto and Iruka, but is repelled by the Kage Bunshin technique and his plot ends in failure.

Yoshino Nara

The mother of Shikamaru. Very strict with her husband and son, but the smiling face she occasionally displays is charming.

Ishi Tatami

A proctor of the Chunin trials. Ishi forms a group with Raido, Shizune, and Genma while working.

Suzume

An instructor of the kunoichi (female ninja) class at the ninja academy. Her education policy is "Clearly, correctly, and beautifully!"

Kotetsu Hagane

Works as a proctor during the Chunin trials the first time Naruto competes. Kotetsu often does things together with Izumo, and is the secretary of the Fifth Hokage Tsunade. During the battle with Kakuzu and Hidan of Akatsuki, Kotetsu produces from a scroll a large hammer-like weapon with a chain attached and fights.

Yugao Uzuki

The lover of Hayate Gekko, she refers to Kakashi as her mentor. She is very single-minded. Her hobby is moon-gazing. She conceals her sorrow over losing Hayate with a mask and continues to carry out her duties.

Konohamaru

The grandson of the Third Hokage and the nephew of Asuma Sarutobi. His parents died in battle with the Nine Tailed Demon Fox. Since he was very young, he has used high-level Henka (Transformation) jutsu, and by doing so shows signs of future talent. He is now a Genin, but is studying the Kage Bunshin (Shadow Clone) jutsu.

Moegi

A member of the Konohagakure military and a Genin. Moegi adoringly refers to Naruto as "Leader."

Udon

A member of the Konohagakure military and a Genin.

Obito Uchiha

A Chunin from the Uchiha clan who serves in a three-man team with Kakashi and Rin. Obito has a passionate sense of camaraderie but his actual ability is meager, and has a complex about being a member of the Uchiha clan. He has a lot of quarrels with the genuinely competent Kakashi. However, his bond with Kakashi ultimately strengthens. During battle, he is killed by his enemy's jutsu and right before he dies passes the Sharingan on to Kakashi. His name is now engraved in a monument, and Kakashi is often late because he never fails to drop by the monument whenever he goes out.

Rin

A kunoichi (female ninja) who forms a team with Obito and Kakashi. She is proficient at healing jutsu. She gives Kakashi a special personal medical pack embroidered with an omamori ("talisman"). She is fond of Kakashi.

Jiraiya

The teacher of Naruto and one of the three legendary ninja. He was also the teacher of the Fourth Hokage. He is the author of "Make Out Paradise," of which Kakashi is a devoted reader. Perhaps, because he has no interest in managing the village, he is usually roaming about traveling (he claims that he is "doing research"). He is recommended for the role of Hokage by the Third Hokage, but because he refuses, the Third Hokage returns to the role. He specializes in summoning jutsu through which he calls forth frog monsters.

Tonton

The pet of Tsunade and Shizune. Tonton has a much better sense of smell than ninja dogs. He is not a summoning beast but a mere pig, and therefore cannot talk.

Nawaki

A former Genin and the little brother of Tsunade. On his 12th birthday, Tsunade gives him a necklace that belonged to his uncle the First Hokage. However, he is killed mysteriously the next day in the line of duty. He dreams of being a Hokage.

Dan

A former Jonin and Tsunade's greatest love. He is the uncle of Shizune. He is given a necklace by Tsunade, but he is killed in the line of duty before Tsunade's eyes. Like Nawaki, he dreams of becoming a Hokage.

Homura Mitokado

A Goikenban (advisor) of the same generation as the first Hokage. He wears glasses. Is a disciple of the First and Second Hokage.

Kohara Utatane

Like Homura, he is a Goikenban of the same generation as the first Hokage. He is a disciple of the First and Second Hokage.

Sakumo Hatake

The father of Kakashi. He has a white sword that fires rays of white light. He is known in every country by his nickname "The White Fang of Konoha." He was a brilliant ninja who could have outshone the three legendary ninja (Tsunade, Jiraiya and Orochimaru). While infiltrating enemy territory 21 years prior to the story arc, he is faced with the choice of either executing his duty or saving the lives of his comrades. He opts for the latter and, as a result, is vilified by his fellow villagers in the Land of Fire, including those he rescued. This causes him so much anguish that he commits suicide. His way of life and his success in battle are kept alive and talked about today in legend. He seems to have greatly resembled Kakashi.

Teuchi

The owner of the ramen shop Ichiraku. Teuchi is one of the few who has seen the true face of Kakashi. Perhaps because Naruto has been frequenting Teuchi's shop since he was small, rather than dislike Naruto like most of the townsfolk, he is friendly to him and occasionally offers him things on the house.

Ayame

The beloved daughter of Teuchi, the owner of the ramen shop Ichiraku. Like her father, she has seen Kakashi's real face, and is enraptured by it. At one time she was quite fat.

Fugaku Uchiha

The father of Itachi and Sasuke. He is the former police chief of Konohagakure. He has a very strong sense of responsibility but is murdered by Itachi.

Mikoto Uchiha

The mother of Itachi and Sasuke. She is murdered by Itachi.

Inabi Uchiha

A member of the Konoha Keimu Butai (Military Police Force). He keeps an eye on Itachi after noticing his odd statements and actions, but, unable to stop Itachi's rampage, he is killed.

Tekka Uchiha

A member of the Konoha Keimu Butai (Military Police Force) and a colleague of Inabi. He views Itachi with hostility.

Shisui Uchiha

Nicknamed "Shunshin (Body Flicker)

Shisui." She is adored by Itachi, but he kills her and makes it look like a suicide in order to get the Mangekyo Sharingan (Kaleidoscope Copy Wheel Eye).

Yashiro Uchiha

A member of the Konoha Keimu Butai (Military Police Force) and a colleague of Inabi and the others. He views Itachi with hostility.

Uruchi Uchiha

The wife of the proprietor of the Uchiha Senbei (rice crackers) store. She is killed when Itachi Uchiha absconds.

Madara Uchiha

The founder of the Uchiha clan. It's said that he was killed at the Valley of the End by the First Hokage.

Sunagakure: The Village Hidden in the Sand (The Land of Wind)

Gaara

A ninja of Sunagakure and the last child of the Fourth Kazekage. He was born as a jinchuriki carrying the Shukaku. Because of his displays of cruelty, he has nearly been assassinated many times and has come to mistrust people. He ordinarily carries sand in a gourd on his back that defends him. If Gaara is attacked, the sand protects him, and because of this, Gaara is said to have Zettai Bogyo

(Absolute Defense). He becomes the Fifth Kazekage. After he is kidnapped by Akatsuki and the spirit of the Shukaku is taken out of him, he dies, but is brought back to life thanks to Chiyobaa's resurrection jutsu.

Temari

A ninja of Sunagakure and the sister of Gaara and Kankuro. Using the wind she creates with her giant fan as a weapon, she mows down enemies in one fell swoop.

Kankuro

A ninja from Sunagakure. He is the brother of Gaara and Temari. A specialist in Kairai (Puppet) jutsu, he fights with enemies by manipulating the excellent puppets made by Sarin.

Third Kazekage

Said to be the strongest Kazekage in history. He can change chakra into magnetic force, which he uses to manipulate iron sand (not unlike Shukaku and his ordinary sand). One day, he suddenly disappears from the village. In fact, he is dead, killed by Sarin (who flees the village). When Chiyobaa confronts Sarin, Sarin uses the Third Kazekage as a human puppet.

Fourth Kazekage

The father of Temari, Kankuro and Gaara. He is assassinated by Orochimaru before the Chunin trials. During the time of the daimyo's military reduction policy, he plotted to make the village more powerful even if it meant sacrificing his wife Karura and his son Gaara (note: it is unclear if Gaara, Kankuro and Temari are maternally related). The Kazekage and Gaara seem to have had an awful father-son relationship in light of Kazekage having plotted Gaara's assassination.

Baki

A Jonin from Sunagakure and a leader of the village. He led Gaara, Temari and Kankuro into the village of Konohagakure. He is called sensei (teacher) by Temari. He is a very reliable man of ability. He kills the Konoha ninja Hayate Gekko when Hayate seems about to discover the plan to destroy Konoha. He performs duties such as keeping an eye on Gaara. He is a specialist in Wind Release jutsu.

Karura

The mother of Gaara (it is unclear whether she is the mother of Temari and Kankuro). It is said that she cursed the village and died at the same time she gave birth to Gaara.

Yashamaru

A healing ninja from Sunagakure. He is the little brother of Karura, making him the uncle of Gaara. He is the protector of Gaara. Gaara feels that Yashamaru is the only one who cares about him. In truth, he hates Gaara, who robbed his sister of her life when he was born. Yashamaru tries to assassinate Gaara after receiving the order to do so from the Fourth Kazekage,

but he is met with an enraged Gaara counterattack and is killed.

Satetsu

A Jonin of Sunagakure. He has a skinhead. He is shocked along with Baki and others when they see the dead body of the Fourth Kazekage.

Otokaze

A Jonin of Sunagakure. In times of emergency he summons his allies by blowing on a small flute he carries. He discovers the completely changed bodies of the Fourth Kazekage and summons Baki, Satetsu and the others. He is the preeminent collector of flutes in the village.

Sajin

A Chunin of Sunagakure. He has only recently been promoted and is still a little wet behind the ears. During the downfall of Konoha, he has a run-in with Shikaku Nara, whose jutsu mops up the floor with Sajin.

Komaza

A Genin of Sunagakure who competes in the Chunin trials. He gets a little too clever for his own good and flunks the trials because of his cheating. Komaza becomes angry with the proctor Tonbo Tobitake (when the reverse should have been true) and Tonbo becomes exasperated.

Nejiri

A Genin of Sunagakure who enters the Chunin trials.

Yura

A Jonin and leader of the village of Sunagakure. He is relied upon by those around him, but is actually a flunky of Akatsuki's Sasori. He dies when his body is used by Akatsuki as a sacrifice for the Shoten (Shapeshifting) jutsu.

Chiyobaa

An advisor of the village of Sunagakure. She is a living link who serves to tie Sunagakure with its allies and other villages. She is a puppeteer who does battle by manipulating puppets. She is the aunt of Sasori of Akatsuki. She is usually spaced out, which worries her little brother Ebizo, but if there is combat she shows physical prowess one wouldn't consider possible in an aged person. As the envoy of Konoha, she conducts great puppet battles, and wins even if they are difficult. For the sake of reviving Gaara (who died when the Shukaku left him), she resigns herself to death and uses the Tensei (Resurrection) jutsu. She entrusts the future of ninja to Naruto and the others, then quietly departs this world.

Ebizo

An advisor of the village of Sunagakure. He is the little brother of Chiyobaa.

Otogakure: The Village Hidden in Sound (The Land of Rice Fields)

Orochimaru

One of the three legendary ninja. He is a former ninja of Konoha and the founder of the village of Otogakure. His parents died when he was still a child. In the time of his training, he studied under Sarutobi (who became the Third Hokage) alongside Tsunade and Jiraiya. Ever since he was little his ninja ability has been outstanding, and for some decades much has been expected of him because of this talent. His ability actually exceeds that of a normal ninja in some respects, and even the genius ninja Kakashi cannot hide his shock when he duels with Orochimaru.

When it comes time to choose the Fourth Hokage, he asserts that he himself is the man for the job. However, because of his twisted thoughts, he is passed over for the position. After that, he begins performing experiments on living people for the sake of developing ninjutsu, but leaves the village after his activities are repressed by Sarutobi. He is, temporarily, a member of Akatsuki, and forms a team in combination with Sasori. He acquires a jutsu through which he is able to replace the mind of another person with his own, and tries to make immortality possible.

His last and probably third host is Gen'yumaru. There seems to be some resistance by his current body and Orochimaru is handicapped during drawn-out battles. It is necessary for him to wait three years before taking over another body. He targets Sasuke's body as the next destination for his soul, and captures him in another dimension created for this purpose. However, he is done in by Sasuke's eye technique and it is Orochimaru whose body is taken over. At present, part of his remains have been transplanted into Kabuto's body, and are gradually eating away at Kabuto.

Kabuto Yakushi

Orochimaru's aide-de-camp. He is a medic ninja of Otogakure. Originally a ninja from Konohagakure, early on he betrays the village and infiltrates Konoha as a spy.

Yoroi Akado

A ninja from the village of Otogakure. Like Kabuto, he infiltrates Konohagakure as an Otogakure spy. He has a black lens on his hood. He is both older than Kabuto and outranks him as a spy, but feels anxiety about Kabuto's actual ability. Kabuto himself points this out and makes a fool of Yoroi. Yoroi has the ability to absorb chakra. At the preliminary third exam of the Chunin trials, he engages in combat with Sasuke. Yoroi uses his ability in close combat to make Sasuke suffer, but ends up being eliminated by Sasuke's latent power.

Misumi Tsurugi

A colleague of Yoroi Akado and Kabuto Yakushi. Like Kabuto and Yoroi, he infiltrates Konohagakure as a spy, and has a round lens on his hood. Also, like Yoroi, Kabuto makes light of him. He is a cold and cruel person. His body has a nature that allows him to dislocate his joints to warp and extend his limbs, enabling him to enter various places to gather information.

Gen'yumaru

The sole survivor of the cruel bloodbath that came about as the result of determining who would be the next vessel for Orochimaru's soul. Gen'yumaru prays to become the next vessel in exchange for the liberation of his clan, which is suffering under Orochimaru. When Orochimaru can't get his hands on Sasuke, he transfers his soul into Gen'yumaru's body.

Kinuta Dosu

With his face covered in bandages, he is the leader of three Genin. He is cold and bellicose, but also calmly decorous. He can amplify the sound his weapon the Kyomeisen (Vibrating Sound Drill) emits, control it with chakra, and attack the sensory perception of his enemies. When he, Kin and Zaku attack Kabuto Yakushi, he uses his sound attack to shatter Kabuto's lens.

Zaku Abumi

A youth who loses his arm in a fight with Shino Aburame at the Chunin trial preliminaries. Through holes punched in his arms, he can emit and attack with wind or supersonic waves. During a childhood of extreme poverty, he is discovered by Orochimaru and becomes a ninja of Otogakure. He is self-confident and loves to fight, but is rather emotional. He has strong feelings of loyalty to Orochimaru, and considers this his reason for existing. In the battle between the Third Hokage and Orochimaru, Orochimaru uses the resurrection jutsu Edo Tensei (Impure World Resurrection); Zaku becomes the vessel for the soul of the Second Hokage and loses his life for the sake of Orochimaru's ambitions.

Kin Tsuchi

A female ninja of Otogakure who has long hair that extends all the way down to her heels. Her character is treacherous, ruthless and extremely jealous. She is envious of Sakura's hair, which is more beautiful than her own, and in the Forest of Death she grabs Sakura's hair and chases her down (this serves as the impetus for Sakura's bobbing of her hair). In the preliminary final exam of the Chunin trials, she uses a bell and needles in a combination attack targeting both the body and the senses, but she meets her match in the form of the Kage Mane (Shadow Copy) jutsu and is eliminated. In the battle between the Third Hokage and Orochimaru, Orochimaru uses the Edo Tensei (Impure World Resurrection) jutsu; Kin's body becomes the vessel for the spirit of the First Hokage and, like Zaku, loses her life for the sake of Orochimaru's ambitions.

The Sound Four (Sound Five including both Sakon and Ukon)

Tayuya

One of the Sound Four. She is given a cursed seal by Orochimaru. She usually has an expressionless "poker face." With the sound of her flute, she summons souls that take on the form of physical matter, and attacks using them or genjutsu. Her only weapon is her magic flute. She has quite the potty mouth, and is often reprimanded by Jirobo. She uses her genjutsu to bring Shikamaru to the extreme limits of suffering, but Temari comes to his rescue. Tayuya battles Temari and loses due to Temari's summoning jutsu Kiri Kiri Mai (Quick Beheading Dance).

Kidomaru

One of the Sound Four. He is given a cursed seal by Orochimaru. He has six arms, three eyes, and can spin thread from his mouth like a spider. This thread is made by combining his special bodily fluids with chakra. It is finer than wire, nearly invisible, sticky and so strong that two elephants cannot pull it apart. He can attack and defend using hardened thread from the spiders he summons. He also uses a bow and arrow.

Sakon

One of the Sound Four. He is given a cursed seal by Orochimaru. Ordinarily, his older brother Ukon is sleeping inside

Sakon, but during battles Ukon emerges to help. Ukon can extend his hands and feet from anywhere within Sakon's body to attack and defend, and can also fight totally separate from him. These abilities are known as the Soma no Ko (Double Demon Attack) Kekkei Genkai.

Sakon has a merciless nature, and a way of fighting in which he wears his opponent down bit by bit. In battle with Kiba, he is wounded in the eye and unable to fight. This is when Kankuro's puppet Kuroari appears and skewes Sakon's body with his Kurohigi Kiki Ippatsu (Black Secret Technique Machine One Shot) jutsu, killing Sakon.

Ukon

One of the Sound Four. He is given a cursed seal by Orochimaru. He usually sleeps within the body of his little brother Sakon, but comes out and helps in times of battle. He has an even more brutal and malicious nature than Sakon, and has a special assassin ability that he uses to turn himself into dust and infiltrate his enemies' body. He fights Kiba, but is injured. Kankuro finishes him off.

Jirobo

One of the Sound Four. He is given a cursed seal by Orochimaru. He can absorb the chakra of enemies. He uses destructive taijutsu attacks. He considers the chakra he absorbs from his enemies to be part of his diet, and is a glutton whose stomach always seems to be empty. Among the Sound Four's members he is the calmest, coolest, and most

collected, and has the most common sense. He is always getting on Tayuya's case for her foul mouth. He contemptuously refers to Choji as the dregs of the five-man Sasuke recovery team, but is defeated thanks to Choji's secret gan'yaku (pill) technique Chodan Bakugeki (Butterfly Bullet Bomb).

Kimimaro

Was kidnapped by Orochimaru when he was small. Since then, he has revered Orochimaru and would even die for Orochimaru. He is the only person who has ever stopped Jugo's attacks. He is the last surviving member of the Kaguya clan, who had the Shikotsumyaku (Corpse Bone Pulse) Kekkei Genkai, which enables them to freely manipulate the bones within their bodies. Kimimaro is the possessor of mysterious skills that even Orochimaru is jealous of. When he became the next candidate for the vessel to be inhabited by Orochimaru's soul, he receives from Orochimaru a cursed earth seal, but he loses all value as such a candidate when he is stricken with a terminal illness. However, thanks to Kabuto Yakushi's strategy he is forced into a fight with Naruto, Rock Lee and Gaara. Ultimately, he dies a very sick man.

Kirigakure: The Village Hidden by Mist (The Land of Water)

Zabuza Momochi

A nukenin from Kirigakure. He made his name as an expert of Buin Satsujin (Silent Killing) jutsu in the former Kirigakure Anbu. He killed all his fellow classmates during the graduation exams for his ninja school. He is one of the greats of Kirigakure (The Seven Swordsmen of the Mist), but after a failed coup following the assassination of the Mizukage, he flees with his underling Haku to become a nukenin. He ordinarily carries a massive kubikiri (currently carried by Suigetsu). He has his mouth wrapped up in bandages, and beneath his cruel facial expressions he carries grandiose ambitions.

Zabuza specializes in Water Release jutsu, and his taijutsu and ninjutsu skills are excellent, arguably making him the equal of Kakashi. He uses his trusty retainer Haku as a tool, although he anguishes over whether to act like a typical ninja or show Haku warmth; this shows that he also has some humanity. Though he is badly injured, Zabuza kills his former employer Gato when Gato mocks the death of Haku, but is then himself abruptly killed by a Gato underling. Zabuza and Haku are buried together in the Land of Water.

Haku

The faithful companion of Zabuza, who has been taught by Zabuza ever since he was taken in as a child. He has an extraordinarily gentle nature and is as quiet as the snow, but he usually follows Zabuza faithfully and gives no quarter to those who would do his master harm. He works as an oinin after Zabuza plans to assassinate the Mizukage, and develops an exhaustive knowledge of the structure of the human body. He attacks using a needle-like weapon called a senbon. He is the user of a Kekkei Genkai known as the Hyotan (Ice Release) ninjutsu, which allows its user to perform elemental recomposition combining water and wind to create ice. As a user of this technique, he has concocted a secret technique using kirifua cards called the Makyo Hyosho (Demonic Ice Mirrors). He has a brilliant mind that enables him to analyze techniques and create countermeasures.

Haku has a tragic past in that he lost his parents because of their Kekkei Genkai. He sincerely admires Zabuza, who sees the value in Haku's "cursed blood" and gives him recognition. He obediently works as Zabuza's subordinate but never really finds out how Zabuza actually feels.

Gozu

An underling of Zabuza and a former Chunin of Kirigakure. The eldest of the Demon Brothers, Gozu is cold and brutal. His special weapon is a blade attached to a chain. Tries to assassinate Tazuna, but unfortunately for Gozu he is beaten back by Kakashi and fails.

Meizu

An underling of Zabuza and a former

Chunin of Kirigakure. The youngest of the Demon Brothers, he has a savage nature. Tries to assassinate Tazuna, but unfortunately for Meizu he is beaten back by Kakashi and fails.

Haku's mother

Hides the fact that she is of a cursed family and has the abhorred Kekkei Genkai. She marries, but is killed when her husband later finds out that she concealed her true nature.

Haku's father

He kills his wife when he finds out that she is part of a line carrying a Kekkei Genkai.

He then tries to do the same with Haku, but Haku awakens to his own Kekkei Genkai and Haku's father is the one who ends up dead.

Hebi (Snake)

Suigetsu

He becomes a follower of Sasuke when he recognizes Sasuke's power after he rescues him. Originally from Kirigakure and one of the Demon Brothers, Suigetsu is locked up in Orochimaru's prison. Suigetsu is a prodigy who is referred to as the second coming of Zabuza, and is also known as such to Akatsuki's Kisame Hoshigaki. He refers to Zabuza as his forerunner, but since he stole the great kubikiri sword (which was used in place of a tombstone) from Zabuza's grave under the pretext of "inheriting" it, it is questionable if he actually reveres Zabuza. When he kills someone, he favors a style in which he chops off the hands and feet first, saving the beheading for last. However, ever since joining Snake, he has followed Sasuke's command to simply go for the vitals (though Suigetsu is a bit dissatisfied with this). In battle he can make part or all of his body transform into liquid (it is unclear if this is a jutsu or just the nature of his body).

Karin

Karin is the favorite of Sasuke and works alongside him. She is the supervisor of Orochimaru's southern base prison. Her manner of speaking is crude. She is the type of girl who acts before she speaks. She has great investigative abilities, and for this she is recruited into Snake. Her attitude toward Sasuke is clearly different from those of the other members.

Jugo

He follows Sasuke to make sure he is worthy of being the carrier of Kimimaro's spirit. He originally had a gentle, quiet nature, but within his mind lies hidden the curious impulses of an assassin. He can't control these impulses, and so voluntarily becomes the subject of human experiments in the northern base. While Kimimaro is still alive, Jugo tells him that he is the only person who can curb his murderous impulses; this is also tied in with his reasons for following Sasuke. According to Karin, Jugo is the one and only origin of the cursed seals, and that the cursed seals given to the Sound Four by Orochimaru were made using Jugo's bodily fluids. Because of this, he has a greater variety of ways of using cursed seals than Sasuke and the Sound Four (e.g., changing parts of his body into special forms, having the cursed seal function so that it affects auditory perception and enables him to convey his will to small animals, etc.).

Iwagakure: The Village Hidden Among Rocks (The Land of Earth)

Kakko

A Jonin from Iwagakure. He forms a group with Taiseki and Mahiru. Kokko is the most able ninja in Iwagakure. Slays Obito Uchiha but dies after Kakashi puts a stop to him.

Taiseki

A Jonin of Iwagakure. He forms a group with Kakko and Mahiru. He had a scary face, but is cool, calm and collected. An effective user of Meisaigakure (Camouflage Concealment) jutsu, he wounds Kakashi in the left eye, but after being gazed upon by Obito's Sharingan (Copy Wheel Eye) he dies.

Mahiru

A Jonin of Iwagakure. He forms a group with Kakko and Taiseki. He is a user of swords. While on reconnaissance he has a run in with the Yellow Flash of Konoha (at the time a Jonin, but later the Fourth Hokage). Though he wounds Kakashi in the fight, he is caught by the Yellow Flash's Hiraishin (Flying Thunder God) jutsu and dies.

Shibito Higashi

A Jonin of Iwagakure. Leading thousands of ninja, he chases down the four remaining members of Konoha but is killed by the Fourth Hokage (who is a Jonin at the time).

Sumashi

A special Jonin of Iwagakure. He is a man of ability with an indifferent expression. He puts together reinforcements and hunts down Kakashi and the others, but is completely destroyed by the Fourth Hokage.

Kumogakure: The Village Hidden Among Clouds (Land of Lightning)

Yugito Nii

A Kumogakure ninja who has the Two Tailed Devil Cat within her body. Captured by Kakuzu and Hidan of Akatsuki, she dies when the Two Tailed Devil Cat is ripped from her body.

Land of Waves

Tazuna

A bridge builder from the Land of Waves who looks out for Naruto and the others in Team Seven. He tries building a bridge to revitalize the obstructed flow of trade in order to bring hope to his country. He has some of the traits of a determined troublemaker, and does things like pretend a task is more difficult than it is in order to gain the assistance of others. Team Seven is also actively involved in the bridge's construction, and it goes without a hitch. After the bridge is complete, Tazuna names it the Great Naruto Bridge in honor of Naruto's active participation as well as his success in opening the hearts of Inari and the people of the island.

Inari

The grandchild of Tazuna. After his beloved stepfather Kaiza is killed, Inari shuts his heart to the world. However, his meeting with Naruto has a great effect on him, and he rises up alongside the people of the island to defend their country.

Tsunami

The mother of Inari and the daughter of Tazuna. She is taken hostage by Zori and Waraji to protect Inari.

Kaiza

The stepfather of Inari. He is originally from another country. Is known as the hero of the nation, but is executed by Gato.

Giichi

A colleague of Tazuna who is active in the building of bridges. He withdrew from bridge-building, citing the physical risk, but returned to his trade for the sake of protecting the country.

Gato

A magnate who operates the ocean shipping firm known as the Gato Company. In reality, he is the boss of an evil organization that deals in narcotics and other contraband, and even plots the takeover of other enterprises and entire nations. He takes over the Land of Waves and cuts off the flow of goods. He hires the nukenin Zabuza and plots the assassination of Tazuna, who intends to build a bridge. Zabuza suffers a fatal wound in a fight with Kakashi. Gato betrays Zabuza, but before Gato can escape, he is killed in a surprise attack by Zabuza using his kunai.

Zori

Bodyguard of Gato. Zori makes off with Tsunami, and tries to kill Inari (who has come to rescue Tsunami), but is caught by Naruto, who had rushed to the scene.

Waraji

A colleague of Zori and a bodyguard of Gato. Waraji is a user of iai (art of drawing one's sword, cutting down one's opponent and then immediately sheathing the sword). He is a heartless man. Like Zori, he is caught by Naruto.

Amegakure: The Village Hidden in the Rain (The Land of Rivers)

Shigure

A Genin from Amegakure who participates in the Chunin trials with Baiu and Midare. He is ridiculed by Gaara as "the old man from Amegakure." He charges at Gaara during the second of the Chunin trials but is killed by Gaara's Sabaku Soro (Desert Funeral) jutsu.

Baiu

A Genin from Amegakure who participates in the Chunin trials with Midare and Shigure. Baiu has a small physique but is the wielder of superhuman strength. He is also killed by Gaara's Sabaku Soro (Desert Funeral) jutsu.

Midare

A Genin from Amegakure who participates in the Chunin trials alongside Baiu and Shigure and is the brains of the trio. Like his friends, Midare shuffles off this mortal coil thanks to Gaara's Sabaku Soro (Desert Funeral) jutsu.

Kagari

A Genin from Amegakure. Kagari forms a three-man cell with Mubi and Oboro in the Chunin trials, but is defeated by Naruto and the others in Team Seven, and the Book of Heaven is snatched back from the trio.

Mubi

A Genin from Amegakure. Mubi forms a three-man cell with Kagari and Oboro in the Chunin trials, but is defeated by Naruto and the others in Team Seven, and the Book of Heaven is snatched back from the trio.

Oboro

A Genin from Amegakure. Oboro forms a three-man cell with Mubi and Kagari in the Chunin trials, but is defeated by Naruto and the others in Team Seven.

Akatsuki members

Pein

The alleged leader of Akatsuki. As the chief of Amegakure, he is revered as a god. After becoming an orphan in the Great Ninja World War, along with Konan, he was taken in by Jiraiya. Jiraiya cared for him for three years and taught him ninjutsu. He has a special Rinnegan (Transmigration Eye) jutsu, and there is speculation that he may be a descendent of Sennin Rikudou (the legendary ninja who developed the foundation of all ninjutsu).

Konan

A woman who works with Pein. When she became an orphan along with Pein, they were taken in and brought up by Jiraiya. Since she is an origami master, she specializes in jutsu that use paper.

Itachi Uchiha

A nukenin from Konohagakure and the older brother of Sasuke. He has the Mangekyo Sharingan (Kaleidoscope Copy Wheel Eye), an extreme version of his clan's Kekkei Genkai, the Sharingan (Copy Wheel Eye). Only a few members of his clan have developed it. He has also mastered the extremely top-secret Amaterasu (Heavenly Light) jutsu.

When he was seven, he was his class valedictorian at the Konohagakure academy. At the age of eight he awakened his Sharingan, and at 10 he became a Chunin. After that, he was accepted into Anbu. When he was 13 he worked as a commander of Anbu. He despises the ties to his family because he feels they hold him back. So he slaughters his clan and leaves the village.

After that, he works as a member of Akatsuki, teamed up with Kisame Hoshigaki. He is the ultimate ninja. He performs high level jutsu other than the Sharingan and is especially skilled with genjutsu. He can put genjutsu into action by merely moving one finger. Because he is part of the Uchiha line, he also specializes in Fire Release jutsu.

Kisame Hoshigaki

A nukenin from Kirigakure. He is wanted for such crimes as murdering the Land of Water's daimyo and plotting an overthrow of the country. A former member of the Seven Swordsmen of the Mist, he is known as Kirigakure's "man of mystery." As his name suggests, he looks like a shark. He often shows up around Konohagakure as he and Sasuke are trying to get their hands on Naruto's Nine Tailed Demon Fox.

Deidara

A nukenin from Sunagakure. He has blue eyes and blonde hair. His left eye, which has a scope attached to it, is concealed by his hair. On the palms of both hands he has holes from which he emits clay mixed with chakra. He uses a technique called the Kibaku Nendo (Exploding Clay), through which he makes various forms and infuses them with chakra. He can increase the amount of infused chakra from levels ranging from C1 to C4. As a self-styled artiste, he claims he creates bombs so he can appreciate the ephemeral beauty of explosions.

He was recruited into Akatsuki by Itachi. However, in the world of illusion created by Itachi's Sharingan (Copy Wheel Eye), he sees what he considers to be "true art". Paradoxically, he begins to resent Itachi and his Sharingan.

He often argued with his former partner Sasori over their conflicting aesthetic viewpoints. After the death of Sasori, he works together with the new recruit Tobi, but Tobi is always giving the irascible

Deidara a hard time.

Sasori

A nukenin from Sunagakure. When he was affiliated with Sunagakure, he was known as a master craftsman of the puppeteer corps. He normally fights after entering the body of a puppet named Hiruko. He can manipulate over 100 puppets at once. He also made Kankuro's three puppets (Karasu, Sanshouo and Kuroari). He is the only person who can reanimate human beings into puppets. He has a collection of people he has killed and made into puppets. One of them is the Third Kazekage (who was the strongest Kazekage in history). Because he has made his own body into a puppet, he looks just like he did the day he left Sunagakure, and will never age. He fights a great, prolonged puppet battle with Chiyobaa and Sakura Haruno. In the battle, his love for his relative Chiyobaa causes him to hesitate when he attacks, and in the end he dies. It is not clear why the ingenious Sasori left Sunagakure to join Akatsuki.

Zetsu

Nothing is known about his past before joining Akatsuki. The left and right sides of his body have different hair and skin colors, and their personalities also differ. The white, left half of his body is kindly and forthright, but the black, right half is grave and speaks haltingly. He has the special ability of eating people and absorbing their power.

The fundamental rule of Akatsuki is that its members must work in groups of two. However, Zetsu alone can work independently. It is thought that this is because he supervises Akatsuki members.

Hidan

A nukenin from parts unknown. His attacks are the slowest among the Akatsuki members, but when it comes to close combat, he is equal to Kakashi Hatake and Asuma Sarutobi.

He is a believer in a cult that has slaughter as its precept. He is such a fervent believer in this faith that he makes time for its ceremonies before and after each battle. He forms a team with fellow Akatsuki member Kakuzu and kills Yugato (who has the two-tailed beast inside him) and Asuma Sarutobi (a Jonin from Konohagakure).

Hidan uses a special ninjutsu that enables him to direct damage he sustains to an opponent. He is also immortal. He continues to live even if he is stabbed in the heart, decapitated, or bleeds profusely. In battle with Sarutobi Asuma, his head is cut off, but Kakuzu reattaches it for him. In the end, he is defeated by Shikamaru's strategy and buried alive.

Kakuzu

A nukenin from Ryugakure. His usual distinguishing trait is his masking of the area around his mouth with a cloth. He is normally cool, calm and collected. However, when trouble breaks out he becomes murderous, and shows no pity, even to his friends. Because of this violent trait, he has killed all his past partners. He loves money to the extreme, and rather than look for jinchuriki, he gives priority to killing people with bounties on their heads.

Kakuzu can separate parts of his body and manipulate them with black, thread-like objects. He can also reattach severed body parts. With this ability, he is able to reattach Hidan's severed head and Deidara's mutilated right arm. He can extract hearts or chakra from stronger ninja while they are still alive and transplant them into himself. Because of this, he has five hearts including his own. He is struck by Naruto's Wind Release: Spiral Shuriken, which obliterates his entire central nervous system, and he dies.

Tobi

Becomes a member to make up for the loss of the deceased Sasori. He treats his partner Deidara as his senior colleague, but with little respect. He gets on Deidara's nerves by cracking jokes, and has a brazen, impudent character. He calls for Deidara's help in the fight with the three-tailed beast, but he brings the beast down with his own jutsu and shows off just how strong he really is. He usually wears a mask inscribed with a whirlpool pattern and never reveals his face. However, his true identity is thought to be Madara Uchiha, and that Tobi himself is the true string-puller behind Akatsuki.

Summoning Beasts

Dogs

Pakkun

A pug-like ninja dog summoned by Kakashi. It's said that Pakkun is the most reliable ninja dog among those that Kakashi summons.

Buru

A bulldog-like ninja dog summoned by Kakashi. Buru has the largest body and loudest bark of all the ninja dogs summoned by Kakashi.

Toads

Gamabunta

A toad who is always smoking a pipe. He has formed a pact with Naruto and Jiraiya, and once had a similar arrangement with the Fourth Hokage. Gamabunta and Naruto have an odd relationship: the power dynamic is inverted, with Gamabunta seemingly the boss and Naruto apparently his follower. Not even Jiraiya can tell Gamabunta what to do. With his incredible bulk, he can alter the landscape during battle. Gamabunta seems to find the fight between Naruto and Gaara (who had changed into his Shukaku form) bothersome. However, because Gamabunta's son had been rescued, he feels obligated to Naruto and so assists him in the battle.

Gamakichi

First appears when Naruto and Jiraiya screw up their summoning of Gamabunta and call Gamakichi instead. He is Gamabunta's son and, like his father, is strong. He is always craving snacks, though what he actually wants to eat is a mystery. He is about the same size as an ordinary toad and is good at reconnaissance. When he tells Gamabunta that he had been rescued, Gamabunta changes his attitude and joins the fight against the Shukaku.

Gamatatsu

Son of Gamabunta and the little brother of Gamakichi. Just like Gamakichi, he is always craving snacks, though what he wants to eat is a mystery. He has a laid-back personality.

Gamaken

A large toad that carries a metal staff.

Giant Snakes

Manda

The most powerful of the giant snakes summoned by Orochimaru. Manda has a violent temper, and it is not easy for even Orochimaru to bring him under control. He seems to reluctantly follow Orochimaru on the condition that he receives human sacrifices. He is acquainted with Gamabunta and Katsuyu, but they are on bad terms and his relationship with Gamabunta is especially strained. At the end of the battle between Deidara and Sasuke, Manda is summoned by Sasuke. He is controlled by Sasuke's genjutsu and is used as a shield against an explosion set by Deidara.

Slugs

Katsuyu

A great slug summoned by Tsunade. Unlike Manda or Gamabunta, she is totally loyal to Tsunade. She is gigantic, even compared with Gamabunta. With her Katsuyu Daibunretsu (Great Slug Division) jutsu, she can divide herself into little slugs.

Monkeys

Enma

An old ape summoned by the third Hokage. The two rely greatly on one another. Enma can turn his body into the adamantium weapon used by the Third Hokage.

Weasels

Kamatari

A one-eyed weasel summoned by Temari. Kamatari's body is small, but he carries a gigantic scythe on his back. He cuts down everything around him when he is summoned by the Kirikiri Mai (Quick Beheading Dance) jutsu.

Tailed Beasts

One Tailed Shukaku
Sealed within Gaara to create a Jinchuriki. It has the form of a monstrous tanuki (raccoon dog). It was once the spirit of an old priest from Sunagakure that was sealed up within a teakettle.

Two Tailed Demon Cat
A tailed beast sealed within the jinchuriki Yugito. It looks like a cat and is the pet of the god of death. It is said to have power over death, and it gathers vengeful spirits.

Three Tails
Takes the form of a turtle. It has three tails and sharply-pointed horns as its distinguishing traits. Because it is not part of a jinchuriki, it is not good at keeping its power under control. It fights with Deidara. It is struck down by Deidara's explosive clay (which is shaped into fish for underwater use) and captured. After that, it is sealed away by Akatsuki.

Four Tails
Sealed away in the body of an old man to create a jinchuriki. It uses lava to melt everything.

Nine Tailed Demon Fox
Sealed in the body of Naruto Uzumaki by the Fourth Hokage when it attacked Konohagakure. The Fourth Hokage lost his life in the process. Previously, it would allot chakra to Naruto in accordance with either Naruto's will or changes in his emotional state. However, recently it seems to be giving out chakra haphazardly as if it has no control over its power.

Ninjutsu

Ninjutsu are the basic techniques used by ninja. Ninja channel chakra from within their bodies, change it into various forms, and use what they have created. Chakra are divided into five categories, depending on their elemental natures: Doton (Earth Release), Katon (Fire Release), Suiton (Water Release), Raiton (Lightning Release), and Futon (Wind Release). However, there are miscellaneous jutsu which do not fit into any of these five categories.

Fire Release

Katon: Kasumi Enbu (Fire Release: Mist Waltz)
User: Kabuto Yakushi

By spraying vaporized gasoline from his or her mouth, the user can turn a small fire and its immediate surroundings into a sea of flames.

Katon: Gamayu Endan (Fire Release: Toad Oil Flame Bullet)
Users: Jiraiya + Gamabunta, Naturo + Gamabunta

Gamabunta vigorously flings oil, and Jiriaya ignites it by breathing fire, increasing the strength of Fire Release techniques.

Katon: Karyudan (Fire Release: Fire Dragon Bullet)
User: Sarutobi, the Third Hokage
Fire is spewed from the user's mouth.

Katon: Karyu Endan (Fire Release: Fire Dragon Flame Bullet)
User: Sarutobi, the Third Hokage

An extremely powerful Fire Release jutsu. Fire is used to attack an opponent dragon-like. Because its flame is manipulated by chakra, it is difficult to dodge.

Katon: Gokakyu (Fire Release: Great Fireball)
Users: Sasuke Uchiha, Obito Uchiha, Itachi Uchiha, Kakashi Hatake

A ball of fire is created and hurled at its target. Members of the Uchiha clan like to use this jutsu.

Katon: Hosenka (Fire Release: Phoenix Immortal Fire)
User: Uchiha Sasuke

Numerous fireballs are breathed out and flung at opponents using chakra. It is also possible to conceal shuriken in the fireballs.

Katon: Zukkoku (Fire Release: Head Mincing Pain)

User: Kakuzu

A jutsu used by monsters created from Kakuzu's body. They emit chakra from their mouths, change the elemental nature into that of fire, and completely incinerate a wide area in one breath.

Katon: Haisekisho (Fire Release: Burning Ash Product)

User: Asuma Sarutobi

Chakra in the body is transformed into superheated ash, which is then expelled from the mouth and explodes.

Katon Hijutsu: Amaterasu (Fire Release Secret Technique: Heavenly Light)

User: Itachi Uchiha

Those who enter the user's field of vision are totally incinerated with black flames. Only those who have developed a Mangekyo Sharingan (Kaleidoscop Copy Wheel Eye) can use it. A great deal of chakra is necessary for its use, and there is the risk that overuse can damage its user's eyesight.

Katon: Hibashiri (Fire Release: Running fire)

User: Shizuku

Both hands and feet are raised and spun, hurling rings of fire. It becomes more powerful if combined with Fire Release techniques.

Katon: Karyu (Dragon Fire)

Users: Uchiha Sasuke, Anko Mitarashi

A jutsu used in conjunction with ningu. Opponents are bound with wire and then ignited. The fire takes the form of a dragon.

Water Release

Kirigakure no Jutsu (Kirigakure Technique)

Users: Zabuza Momochi, Kakashi Hatake

A jutsu that allows the user to create thick mist, then hide within it. If lots of chakra is used it is possible to reduce visibility to nearly zero. It can be used as a diversion in combination with various other jutsu. The ninja of Kirigakure specialize in it.

Suiton: Kokuo (Water Release: Black Rain)

Users: Orobo, Mubi, Kagari

Black oil is brought down like rain. It turns into a great conflagration when ignited.

Suiton: Goshokuzame (Water Release: Five Eating Sharks)

User: Kisame Hoshigake

The user immerses his or her hands in water and sends chakra flowing down into it. Five shark-like entities materialize in the water and attack opponents.

Suiton: Suigadan (Water Release: Water Fang Bullet)
User: Itachi Uchiha

The user fixes his or her gaze on an opponent and sends spinning, compressed demons flying at said counterpart. It is quite lethal, and can also be used in diversionary tactics.

Suiton: Suikodan no Jutsu (Water Release: Water Shark Bullet)
Users: Kisame Hoshigaki, Kakashi Hatake

Water in the shape of a shark rushes towards enemies and drowns them.

Suiton: Suishoha (Water Release: Water Wave)
User: The Second Hokage

Uses chakra to create water, which topples enemies like a tsunami.

Suiton: Suijinheki (Water Release: Water Encampment Wall)
Users: The Second Hokage, Kakashi Hatake

Protects the user by creating a wall of water around his or her body. It is also possible to create walls by spewing water made from chakra from the mouth. Because the water is free of bubbles, it is totally translucent. This jutsu can even be used in places where there is no water.

Suiton: Suiryudan no Jutsu (Water Release: Water Dragon Bullet)
Users: Zabuza Momochi, Kakashi Hatake, the Second Hokage

A great mass of water in the form of a dragon strikes opponents.

Suiton: Daibakufu no Jutsu (Water Release: Great Waterfall)
Users: Zabuza Momochi, Kakashi Hatake

A great mass of water rises up and plunges down like a waterfall. It is powerful enough to gouge out the ground, and the area around it looks like it has suffered a natural disaster.

Suiton: Daibakuryu (Water Release: Great Exploding Current)
User: Yoroi Akado

A great whirlpool is created with the user of the jutsu at the center.

Suiton: Takitsubo (Water Release: Waterfall Basin)
User: Yamato

First, cliffs are created using the Doton Doryu Jouheki (Earth Style Rampart). Water then gushes forth from the top of the cliffs, creating a waterfall.

Suiton: Teppo Dama (Water Release: Gunshot)

Chakra within the body is used to create water, which is then compressed into a sphere and hurled at an opponent. It can be used anywhere, and it is also possible to channel chakra into the water sphere.

Suiton: Bakusui Shoha (Water Release: Exploding Water Shockwave)
User: Kisame Hoshigaki

Chakra in the mouth is changed into a massive quantity of water, which is then spat out with the force of a tsunami. Its user can also ride the water. However, its true advantage is that it can be used even where there is no water to power other Water Release jutsu.

Suiton Hijutsu: Sensatsu Suisho (Water Release: Thousand Flying Water Needles of Death)
User: Haku

By changing water into a huge quantity of needles, the user can attack opponents from a nearly 360-degree range.

Suiro No Jutsu (Water Prison Technique)
Users: Kisame Hoshigaki, Zabuza Momochi

Targets are trapped in spheres of water and are unable to breathe. However, in order to maintain this, the user of the jutsu must continuously touch the spheres with his or her hands.

Mizu Bunshin no Jutsu (Water Clone Technique)
Users: Kisame Hoshigaki, Zabuza Momochi, Kakashi Hatake

Other than the fact that is uses water, it is fundamentally identical to the Kage Bunshin (Shadow Clone) technique. It is relatively easy to master compared with the Kage Bunshin, but the ability of the water clones is inferior to that of the shadow clones.

Wind Release

Kaze no Yaiba (Blade of Wind)
User: Kiba

A vacuum is created extending from the fingers, and the chakra becomes matter that transmogrifies into a powerful blade. This technique was used to defeat Hayate Gekko (a judge of the preliminary third exam of the Chunin trials) with one blow.

Kama Itachi no Jutsu (Cutting Whirlwind Technique)
User: Temari

By using a giant fan to blow chakra into the wind, a vacuum is created that rips things apart.

Kuchiyose: Kirikiri Mai (Summoning: Quick Beheading Dance)
The weasel Kamatari is called forth, and it creates a ferocious slicing whirlwind that cuts anything and everything in its vicinity to pieces.

Futon: Atsugai (Wind Release: Pressure Damage)
User: Kakuzu

A jutsu used by monsters that spring forth from the body. Wind demons create a windy air mass that blows away everything in reach.

Futon: Daitoppa (Wind Release: Great Breakthrough)
User: Orochimaru

A gale is caused by amplifying chakra blown from the mouth.

Futon: Mugen Sajin Daitoppa: Infinite Sand Cloud Great Breakthrough
User: Gaara

The user absorbs air around the body and blasts forth dust-clouded air.

Futon: Rasengan (Wind Release: Spiraling Sphere)
User: Naruto Uzumaki

A jutsu that changes the elemental nature of a spiraling chakra sphere into that of wind. Its development was the goal of the Fourth Hokage. Based on clues from Kakashi, Naruto developed it by having three Kage Bunshin clones work on it in three roles: one worked on changing its shape, one worked on changing its elemental nature, and one worked on channeling chakra to create it. By coming up with this method, Naruto successfully developed the Rasengan.

Futon: Rasen Shuriken (Wind Release: Spiraling Shuriken)
User: Naruto Uzumaki

A kinjutsu that is even more powerful than the Rasengan. Structurally, it has the spiraling sphere as its core and makes a shuriken pattern using chakra. The jutsu is powerful enough to send shockwaves and deafening booms through the surrounding area. It has a secondary phase in which the spiraling sphere develops with its targeted opponent at its center. The wind coating the surface of the spiraling sphere swirls around and the target is enveloped in its turbulence. The opponent is at the center of a convergence of attacks as the spiraling sphere spins violently. By changing the form of its chakra into needles, the user can attack all an opponent's cells. However, because of its great shockwaves, its user can suffer broken bones, and even suffer light damage at the cellular level. Because of this, it is a kinjutsu.

Futon: Renkudan (Wind Release: Drilling Air Bullet)
User: The Shukaku

The user spews out ultra-compressed air by channeling chakra into the air in the abdomen and beating on the belly.

Earth Release

Kuchiyose: Doton: Suiga (Summoning: Earth Release: Tracking Fang)
User: Kakashi Hatake

The user summons four ninja dogs. Relying on their sense of smell, they hunt down opponents. Kakashi developed this himself.

Doton: Iwayado Kuzushi (Earth Release: Rock Lodging Cave-In)
User: Kakko

Causes entire caves to crumble by

disrupting the arrangement of the rocks. It is also possible to cause just one part of a cavern to fall in.

Doton Kekkai: Dorodomu (Earth Release Barrier: Dungeon Chamber of Nothingness)

User: Jirobo

The target of the jutsu is trapped within an earthen dome. Even if one tries to destroy the dome, it automatically repairs itself. It is also possible to rob the victims trapped inside of all their chakra by using the Dorodomu in conjunction with chakra absorption techniques.

Doton: Shinju Zanshu (Earth Release: Inner Decapitation)

User: Kakashi Hatake

A jutsu that buries its target in the ground up to the neck. It was originally used by members of Anbu to facilitate interrogations.

Doton: Dochu Eigyo (Earth Release: Underground Fish Projection)

Users: Orobo, Mubi, Kagari

Fish swim around in the ground like fish swimming underwater.

Doton: Doryu Joheki (Earth Release: Earth Flow Rampart)

User: Yamato

Tall cliffs standing perpendicular to the ground are created right before the user's eyes. This was the jutsu used to explain Seishitsu Henka to Naruto.

Doton: Doryu Taiga (Earth Release: Earth Flowing River)

User: Sarutobi, the Third Hokage

A turbid current sweeps away the opponent.

Doton: Doryudan (Earth Release: Earth Dragon Bullet)

User: Sarutobi, the Third Hokage

Mud changes into the shape of a dragon, which spits out bullets of mud.

Doton: Doryu Heki (Earth Release: Earth Flow Rampart)

A sturdy wall used for self-defense is created with earth spat from the mouth.

Doton: Doryu Dango (Earth Release: Earth Mausoleum Dumpling)

User: Jirobo

An earthen wall is created standing perpendicular to the ground. However, it does not offer defense against very powerful attacks.

Doton: Yominuma

User: Jiraiya

Opponents sink into a bottomless swamp created on the ground around them. The size of the swamp is relative to the quantity of chakra used.

Doton: Retsudo Tenshou (Earth Release: Split Earth Turn Around Palm)

User: Kakko

Fissures are created on the ground. It

is the basic ninjutsu in Iwagakure.

Lightning Release

Chidori (One Thousand Birds)
User: Sasuke Uchiha

Because of the chi-chi-chi noise created by the electric shocks in the user's right hand, this jutsu came to be known as the Chidori. Using all of one's strength, the jutsu is intensified and concentrated into one point, then used to stab. Because of this concentration, it is easy for its user to fall prey to counterattacks no matter how skilled he or she may be. For this reason, Kakashi sealed away the jutsu after he developed it.

Chidori Senbon (One Thousand Birds One Thousand Needles)
User: Sasuke Uchiha

The user transforms the Chidori held in the palm into needles and hurls them.

Chidori Nagashi (One Thousand Birds Current)
User: Sasuke Uchiha

Enemies are paralyzed by Chidori issued from all over the user's body. This jutsu is a development of the original Chidori jutsu.

Raikiri (Lightning Cut)
User: Kakashi Hatake

An original ninjutsu created by the "copy ninja" Kakashi. Originally the Chidori, Kakashi used it to slice through lightning and from it acquired its present name. This jutsu's creation was influenced by the Rasengan (Spiraling Shuriken). It has uses such as piercing the heart of an enemy in close combat after stopping said enemy with electric shocks, using the electric shocks in one or both hands to offset other Lightning jutsu, or cutting through threads and ropes.

Raiton: Gian (Lightning Release: False Darkness)
User: Kakuzu

This jutsu is used by monsters that emerge from the Gian user's body. Chakra converted into lightning is shot from their mouths at great speed. It is accompanied by an extremely dazzling ray of light, and the power of its flash of lightning is about the same as the Raikiri (Lightning Cut).

Keitai Henka

Rasengan (Spiraling Sphere)
Users: Naruto Uzumaki, Jiraiya, Kakashi Hatake, the Fourth Hokage

Chakra is concentrated and spun violently on the palm of the hand, and then used to strike an opponent. Enemies struck by it suffer a spiral-shaped wound, and are sent flying by the force of the spiral. It represents the upper limits of Keitai Henka, and even in its unmodified state boasts terrible power. Because of the complicated chakra controls involved, it is an extremely difficult ninjutsu to master.

Odama Rasengan (Giant Ball Spiraling Sphere)
User: Naruto Uzumaki

Has a terrible power far greater than that of the ordinary Rasengan. It entails attacking enemies using Rasengan in concert with a Kage Bunshin clone.

Kyubi Rasengan (Nine Tails Spiraling Sphere)
User: Uzumaki Naruto

A Rasengan that is formed by collecting the chakra of the Nine Tailed Demon Fox.

Iryo (Medical) Ninjutsu

In'yu Shometsu (Shadow Wound Removal)
User: Kabuto Yakushi

Chakra is accumulated and used to heal wounds when injuries are sustained. Because one has to determine which places will be injured beforehand, it requires precise analytical ability.

Shikon no Jutsu (Dead Soul Technique)
User: Kabuto Yakushi

Used to temporarily resuscitate a corpse's heart and manipulate the corpse, making it appear to be still alive.

Shosen Jutsu (Enchanted Palm Technique)
User: Kabuto Yakushi

Used to hasten the recovery of injuries by applying chakra concentrated on the palm of the user's hand to said wounds. It is also possible to induce sleep by using more chakra than necessary.

Sozo Saisei (Creation Rebirth)
User: Tsunade, the Fifth Hokage

Using immense chakra accumulated on the forehead, the body's metabolism is stimulated and the speed of cell division is increased, shortening the amount of time needed to recover from injuries. Since the activities of cells are greater than usual, lifespan is also decreased. Because of this side effect, the aging process is also accelerated for a while after the use of the jutsu.

Chikatsu Saisei no Jutsu (Healing Resuscitation Regeneration Technique)
User: Shizune

Using the cells of hair and the like as a medium, new cells are created.

Chakra Mesu (Chakra Scalpel)
User: Kabuto Yakushi

A jutsu that uses a scalpel made from chakra as a weapon. This chakra scalpel was originally used in surgery. Because it is difficult to control chakra used in this way, the reach of the chakra scalpel is inevitably short. However, it has the benefit of being able to inconspicuously damage the enemy by severing muscles or nerves without creating external wounds.

Tensei Ninjutsu (Resurrection Ninjutsu)
User: Chiyobaa

A kinjutsu that revives the dead in exchange for the jutsu user's life. In other words, the users of this jutsu all die. This jutsu was developed with the goal of breathing life into puppets, but because of numerous casualties stemming from its use it was banned.

Dokugiri (Poison Mist)

A ninjutsu that changes the chakra in the body into a special chemical substance and expels it through the mouth. When this substance meets air it instantaneously changes into a deadly purple poison. Even if a tiny bit is breathed in, it will surely lead to death.

Fushi Tensei (Living Corpse Reincarnation)

User: Orochimaru

An extreme kinjutsu developed by Orochimaru. It allows its user's soul to be transferred into the body of another person, making immortality possible. However, once it is used, two or three years have to pass before it can be used again.

Ranshinsho (Bodily Confusion Attack)

User: Tsunade, the Fifth Hokage

Floods enemy's central nervous system with electrified chakra, frying his brain and leaving him immobile.

Space-Time Ninjutsu

Kuchiyose no Jutsu (Summoning Techniques)

Users: Naruto Uzumaki, Kakashi Hatake, and others

Jutsu that allow users to summon life forms with which he or she has formed blood pacts. Users of the jutsu can force the summoned life forms to follow them (although in Naruto's case the relationship is reversed due to the great power of the summoned animal). Also, even if one hasn't formed a pact with the summoned life form, it is still possible to put the jutsu into action as long as one has blood of the user and knowledge of the jutsu ceremony.

Kuchiyose: Edo Tensei (Summoning: Impure World Resurrection)

User: Orochimaru

A kinjutsu that brings the dead back to the world of the living. It requires a human sacrifice as a vessel for the souls of the resurrected dead. After resurrection, the area around the bodies of the sacrificial victims is strewn with rubbish, and the bodies take on the appearance the resurrected dead had when they were alive. By implanting a tag on the heads of the bodies, it is possible to make the bodies follow the jutsu user's command when they are resuscitated. Even if the user of the jutsu dies, the jutsu itself does not wear off. Also, the power of the jutsu allows the bodies to quickly heal when they are damaged.

Kuchiyose: Gamaguchi Shibari (Summoning: Toad Mouth Bind)

User: Jiraiya

A jutsu that only summons part of a giant toad's digestive track. Enemies are sucked into this great hunk of flesh, where they are carried down to the stomach and digested.

Kuchiyose: Yataikuzushi no Jutsu (Summoning: Food Cart Destroyer Technique)

User: Jiraiya

A giant toad is summoned. It materializes over an opponent's head, falls, and smashes the opponent.

Kuchiyose: Rashomon (Summoning: Rashomon)

Users: Sakon and Ukon

A giant gate with a sinister engraving is summoned. It is the greatest defense protecting Orochimaru. It is not just sturdy but also highly elastic, and is resilient enough to absorb the Garoga (Double Wolf Fang) attack of Akamaru and Kiba.

Kuchiyose: Sanju Rashomon (Summoning: Triple Rashomon)

User: Orochimaru

An absolute defense that summons three Rashomon. It uses a great deal of chakra.

Hiraishin no Jutsu (Thunder God Technique)

User: The Fourth Hokage

Allows its user to instantaneously move from one place to another. It earned the Fourth Hokage his nickname the Yellow Flash.

Sen'ei Jashu (Hidden Shadow Snake Hand)

Users: Orochimaru, Anko Mitarashi

The enemy is trapped by a snake that is summoned and coils around the enemy.

Sen'ei Tajashu (Hidden Shadow Multiple Snake Hands)

Users: Orochimaru, Sasuke Itachi

The enemy is captured by a massive quantity of summoned snakes.

KEYWORD INDEX

A

Aburame	92
Akamaru	30
Akatsuki	22 73 78 83 89 113 117
	134 137 139 141 149
Amegakure	10 137 139 141 149 95
Anbu	99 101
Anko Mitarash	89 112 122 138
Asuma	20 42 102

B

Baika jutsu	97
Byakugan	95 149
	8 11

C

Chakra	25 31 33 48 56 113 130
Chidori	33
Chiyobaa	109 113 115 117 119
Choji	25 97 130
Choju Giga	99
Chunin	20

D

Danzo	99
Deidara	136 137 143

E

Ebisu	20
Edo Tense	28 64

F

Fourth Hokage	42 44 54 64 122
First Hokage	64 69 146

G

Gaara	10 13 40 46 108 109 111
	115 120 134
Genjutsu	25
Genin	20
Genma Shiranui	21
Goikenban	20 67 69

H

Haku	33
Hanzo	141
Hebi	87 99
Hidan	102 137 145
Hina Hyuga	95
Hokage	62

I

Ino Yamanaka	8 105
Inoichi Yamanaka	8 105
Itachi Uchiha	36 76 78 80 89 136
	137 139
Iwagakure	10

J

Jinchuriki	83 113 127 134 136
Jiraiya	67 69 141 149
Jirobo	130
Jonin	20
Jugo	87
Juin	25

K

Kabuto Yakushi	85 124
Kage Bunshin	28 48 56
Kakashi	20 33 56 81 89 90
	102 109
Kakuseigan	81
Kakuzu	102 137 146
Kankuro	30 33
Karin	87
Kazekage	46 71 108 103 109
Kekkei Genkai	16 25 33 36 64 76
	95 126 145
Kiba Inuzuka	20 30 93
Kidomaru	33 83 127
Kikaichu	25 92
Kimimaro	36 73 87 126

Kirigakure	10 16 22 33 36
	87 136
Kisame Hoshigaki	136 137
Konohagakure	8 10 16 18 42 62 64
	69 71 73 76 78 89 90
	115 122 124 136
Konohamaru	20 102 117 119 120
Kugutsu	117
Kumogakure	10
Kurenai	102
Kusagakure	10

M

Madara Uchiha	139 148
Mangekyo Sharingan	76
Might Guy	20 25

N

Nagato	149
Neji Hyuga	36 95
Nine Tailed Demon Fox	40 42 44 48 50
	52 54 64 78
	134 139 148
Ninjutsu	25

O

Obito Uchiha	90
Orochimaru	10 16 64 67 69 71 73
	80 81 83 85 87 89
	122 124 126 127
	129 136 139

Otokagakure	10 22 73 122 124

P

Pein	141 149

R

Raikage	10
Rasengan	33 46 52 56 59
Rasen Shuriken	56 59
Rock Lee	16 25 50
Rinnegan	149
Rin	90
Ryuugakure	10

S

Sakon	129
Sakumo Hatake	109 115
Sakura	31 69 99
Sai	99
Sasori	117 119 136
	137 139
Sasuke Uchiha	16 31 69 73 80 81
	83 85 87 89 99
	124 126 139
Second Hokage	64
Sennin Rikido	149
Sharingan	25 36 76 85 90
	95 143 148 149
Shikamaru	25 103 129 131
Shiki Fujin	28 64

Shinranshin	105
Shintenshin	105
Shukaku	46 108 113 134
Suigetsu	87
Sunagakure	10 13 46 71 108
	109 115 117 119
	120 136

T

Taijutsu	25
Tayuya	131
Temari	120
Third Hokage	42 69 71 99 102
Tobi	139 148
Tokubetsu Jonin	20
Tsuchikage	10
Tsunade	42 67 69 89

U

Ukon	129
Urarenge	28

Y

Yamato	44

Z

Zabuza	87
Zetsu	137